TALKING
BACK
TO SEXUAL
PRESSURE

TALKING BACK

TO SEXUAL PRESSURE

WHAT TO SAY

...to resist persuasion
...to avoid disease
...to stop harassment
...to avoid acquaintance rape

ELIZABETH POWELL, M.S., M.A.

CompCare® Publishers
Minneapolis, Minnesota

Library of Congress Cataloging-in-Publication Data
Powell, Elizabeth
    Talking back to sexual pressure : what to say, to resist pressure, to avoid disease, to stop harassment, to avoid acquaintance rape / by Elizabeth Powell.
        p.   cm.
    Includes index.
    Summary : Provides advice and specific skills for asserting and protecting your sexual rights, including what to say and do in uncomfortable or potentially dangerous situations, and where to get and give help.
    ISBN 0-89638-239-7
    1. Sex instruction—United States. 2. Assertiveness (Psychology) 3. Verbal self-defense. 4. Sexual harassment—United States—Prevention 5. Rape—United States—Prevention [1. Sex instruction. 2. Assertiveness (Psychology) 3. Sexual harassment—Prevention 4. Rape—Prevention] I. Title.
HQ31.P79   1991
306.7—dc20   90-28272
                                                                  CIP
                                                                   AC

Cover and interior design by MacLean and Tuminelly

Inquiries, orders, and catalog requests should be addressed to:
CompCare Publishers
2415 Annapolis Lane
Minneapolis, Minnesota 55441
Call toll free 800/328-3330
(Minnesota residents 612/559-4800)

  6   5   4   3   2   1
 96   95   94   93   92   91

In memory of my great-grandmother, Eliza Davis,
who survived rape in the aftermath of the Civil War,
this offering for justice.

And for all survivors of sexual exploitation:
May you live to say,
Never again.

CONTENTS

ACKNOWLEDGMENTS

I would like to thank the following people for their patient evaluation and criticism: Mary Angelides, Joseph Dunne, Lee Ehrenberg, Barbara Fine, Peter Griffin, Shari Klein, Barry Schapiro, Sharon Burton Smith, Byron Walker, and Susan Waugh. I am grateful to Joan Hartmann and Margaret Terry for brainstorming. I am also indebted to John Thompson and to Robert Gillespie, my team teacher, for advice on biological matters. Melinda Smith, Rayna Morrison, and Michele Smith are much appreciated for criticisms from the singles viewpoint. I owe a special thanks to Amy Salniker for her very useful comments. I also want to thank Lois Vander Waerdt for her advice on legal issues. I appreciate the generosity of Edward Donnerstein and Dolf Zillmann, among our foremost researchers on sexual aggression in the media, whose phone conversations helped keep me up-to-date on their current research.

I am grateful to my students for sharing their questions and concerns—particularly the role players, whose courage helped me see what skills are needed for sexual safety.

And lastly, thanks to my Kentucky mountain kinfolks from the past and present, people of profound integrity and kindness. I especially cherish the steadfast example of my mother and father, which showed me that it is always possible to treat people right.

This book is written for anyone who wants to know what to say in situations where there is sexual pressure. While young singles are the usual seekers of this kind of information, even people in their forties and fifties may profit from using sexual assertiveness skills suitable for the nineties.

All the examples in this book (except those related to pregnancy) can apply equally well to homosexuals or heterosexuals.
I hope that sexual assertiveness will be used extensively in the gay community.

I will use "he" or "she" interchangeably throughout the book in the interest of helping all readers relate to the examples. Where anecdotes involve real people, their names have been changed.

Although this book contains information about legal and medical issues, that information is not intended as legal or medical advice. To locate an attorney for advice on a specific matter, contact your local bar association or lawyers reference service for a list of licensed attorneys who practice in the area of your concern. To locate a physician, contact your local medical association.

This book also suggests resources where readers can seek help. Many of these are national organizations with local affiliates which may vary in the actual services and the quality of services provided.

Although you may find many suggestions for self protection in this book, no one can forsee the precise circumstances in which you may find yourself. I hope you use this advice to increase your options, but ultimately you must rely on your own judgment as to which options you decide to attempt.

I

HOW TO BECOME ASSERTIVE ABOUT SEX

CHAPTER ONE

Breaking the Silence

If I am not for myself, who will be for me?
If I am only for myself, what am I?
—And if not now, when?

—Hillel

Never before has a society provided so many ways to get into sexual trouble. Our country has the highest teenage pregnancy rate in the Western Hemisphere. Four sexually transmitted diseases have reached epidemic proportions; the most serious of these—Acquired Immune Deficiency Syndrome, or AIDS—has caused thousands of deaths and the virus has infected hundreds of thousands more who do not yet show symptoms. The United States has one of the highest rates of rape in the world: at least one in four American women will be raped in her lifetime. Sexual dysfunctions and even total lack of sexual desire are becoming distressingly common among both males and females. Our children are not sexually safe, sometimes even from their own parents and often from others in whose care they have been placed. One of ten boys and one of five girls are sexually abused before the age of puberty. In short, our country is a sexual disaster area.

Even more remarkable in the face of all these sexual problems, the majority of our citizens consider themselves unable, or unwilling, to talk about the very subjects that could drastically reduce or prevent these problems. Thousands could die and millions more become infected with a deadly disease that is sexually transmitted, but our society is so sexually impaired that many of its politicians, educators, and religious leaders would not so much as mention the kind of protection that could save those lives.

HAZARDOUS RECREATION

The media overwhelm us with a barrage of sexual innuendos, titillation, and jokes, yet leave us without training or knowledge or permission to talk about sexual subjects in a healthy, assertive way. The typical American owns a little electric picture box that runs an average of seven hours a day,[1] and it portrays some of the most manipulative sex to be found anywhere. Take, for example, the soaps. During one month chosen at random, newspaper synopses of weekly soaps described the following:[2]

1. Thirty instances of sexual deception.
Examples: "Emily convinced Paul to keep mum about their liaison because Barbara (and others) wouldn't understand." "Trevor blackmailed Marissa into sleeping with him and secretly made a videotape of their lovemaking."

2. Three instances of rape.
Example: "Cricket agreed to have dinner with Derek, who raped her when she tried to rebuff him."

3. Fifteen incidents of casual sex (not including the deceptions above).
Example: "Jessica spent the night with Rob after they met at an AA meeting."

4. Six instances in which the parentage of a child is uncertain.
Example: "Greg told C.C. that he is going to have a blood test to prove that he is C.C.'s son."

Print media are equally likely to highlight unhealthy sex. Popular novels abound with themes of unsafe, casual sex or sex that treats women as objects. A frequent example is the "stud" male who takes sex wherever he can find it with no regard to feelings, disease, or pregnancy; included in this fantasy is the ever-willing female. We see this in Jackie Collins's *Rock Star*:

"Taking a survey one day, both Kris and Buzz had decided that the easiest girls to have it off with were the English. A quick bit of the verbals and it was up, up, and away. Second were the Scandinavians—Swedish, Danish, and Finnish—easy pickings."[3]

Advertisers also portray unhealthy sex to sell products. In a recent perfume ad that shows a man who is labeled as "Trouble," the caption says, "A fragrance for those times when your better judgment is better off ignored."[4] But better judgment is precisely what we need to encourage.

Unhealthy sex is all around us, flagrantly used to capture our attention and our money. But examples of healthy sex are harder to get than an X-rated film.

If we had been born into a peace-loving, respectful tribe, much of this would not be so. We would not be barraged by constant sexual messages that contradict the healthy messages we need. We would not have to find ways to protect ourselves sexually because very likely no one would attempt to violate our sexual rights. Community standards and group disapproval would squelch an aggressive impulse before it became an action. We still might need to know how to talk about sexual matters, however, either to ask for something we need, to explain something sexual to someone, or to refuse an undesired partner.

THE RISK TO MEN

Men may doubt that they need to know how to deflect sexual pressure, but both men and women need to know what to say to help themselves in a variety of sexual situations. Contrary to popular belief, men are sexually pressured by both male and female employers. Fifteen percent of the males in the federal work force claim to have been sexually harassed on the job.[5] Men are vulnerable to sexually transmitted diseases, and they can impregnate someone with whom they never would have had sex if they had been thinking rationally.

More than that, men pay a high price for living in a society where there is so much sexual exploitation. Many a man feels uncomfortable when, walking behind a woman at night, he notices her speeding up and realizes she is afraid of him. When their daughters, their sisters, their wives, and the women with whom they are involved have been victimized, men also pay a price. What another has done to the woman a man loves may haunt her, and change how she relates to him.

Males suffer, too, for being the "bad guys." Their high rate of sexual crimes against women makes even innocent men appear dangerous, and this fear is exaggerated in the way they are often depicted as sex-driven madmen in the media. Men in this society never know when they are going to be falsely accused of a sexual mistake. Some of my male colleagues (teachers, therapists, and other professionals) are more than a little jittery about the possibility that someone might fabricate a charge against them. What if they are affectionate, and accidentally pat a woman on the back or the hand in an effort to reassure her? Victims of sexual harassment have become more successful in the courts; does this fact mean that innocent men will be prosecuted?

Males are vulnerable to the problems caused by living in a society that cannot deal with sexual matters in a healthy, straightforward way. And even the perpetrators of sex crimes are also victims. They are damaged by our refusal to cope with sex, for in their histories there are invariably critical experiences when sexual assertion could have helped. Many abusers, rapists, exhibitionists, and obscene phone callers have been victimized in some way in childhood, often in their own families. Sexual assertiveness and respect for sexual rights are not often found in such families. A society that took sexual assertiveness for granted might have prevented the chain of abuse.

THE RISK TO WOMEN

Although modern men need to learn sexual assertiveness for a number of reasons, women have been the main victims of sexual exploitation for centuries. My own great-grandmother, to whom this book is dedicated, was a typical example. After the Civil War, when her family's tiny Virginia farm was looted, she went at age fourteen to work on a plantation in Tennessee. There she was sexually harassed and raped by the plantation owner. That man was my great-grandfather. "Granny" later married another man and brought her son over the Cumberland Gap into Kentucky, where our family has lived for over a hundred years. When I knew her, she was a little, stooped woman in a mountain bonnet who lived to be ninety-six. I would never have heard her story except for the fact that my uncle—the youngest of my great-grandmother's twelve grandchildren and an historian—revealed it to me during a visit a few years ago. Granny's story is a common example of the price women have had to pay for their lack of power. Assertion might have helped, but often victims are unable to resist.

To a great extent, powerless people are the chief victims today. In *Human Sexuality*, Masters and Johnson, our foremost sex therapists, say, "We live in a society that trains and encourages females to be victims of sexual coercion and males to victimize females."[6] Part of that training is the message given to American males: Don't be assertive—be aggressive. Take over, be powerful and masterful. And the message to females: Don't be assertive, be nice; you won't be loved if you aren't nice. This kind of background distorts the behavior of a typical couple, making the man aggressive and the woman compliant—a combination that is dangerous because it often ends in sexual abuse.

We need to stop this silence that results in nonassertiveness and sexual harm. We must train our citizens to speak up about sexual concerns, just as we teach them how to drive safely. What was good enough for the forties is not good enough for the exploitive nineties.

WHAT'S IN IT FOR YOU?

If you can be sexually assertive, you can enhance your sexual relationships and protect yourself in innumerable ways. In particular, you can

1. *Decrease, or completely eliminate, your risk of contracting a sexually transmitted disease (STD).* Asserting your needs for information and protection is a basic necessity and responsibility if you are sexually active and are not in a long-standing faithful

relationship. Except in a case of rape, *you* largely control your exposure to STDs.

2. *Decrease your risk of pregnancy or of impregnating someone.* The rate of unwanted pregnancy in nonassertive individuals is far higher than in those who ask for protection. Two-thirds of sexually active American teenagers do not use contraception during their first act of intercourse. When asked why, they often report that they could not speak of such things. Many have intercourse when they don't even feel ready, but can't assert themselves enough to refuse. Well-meaning adults may tell them to "just say no," but they don't know how. Yet many of them can easily use the most graphic sexual words to insult each other.

3. *Decrease your odds of being raped by an acquaintance.* I want to be very careful not to suggest that all sexual victimization could have been avoided or is in some way *caused* by unassertiveness in the victim. Any rape is always the responsibility of the perpetrator, and often the victim could have done nothing to prevent the rape, or else could think of nothing to do under such stress. But when rape by an acquaintance is a threat, the potential victim's assertiveness can sometimes change the balance of power. This effect is important because rape is primarily a crime of anger and power. A rapist's fantasies of a passive partner who says "No" when she means "Yes" are more likely to be discouraged by an assertive attitude in the intended victim. It is for this reason that I include the possibility of learning to use assertiveness in certain sexual situations *before* coercion can happen.

4. *Decrease the odds of being sexually harassed.* Sexual harassment is sexual pressure from someone who has power over you in some way, such as your teacher or employer. Chapter 6 will explain more precisely what constitutes harassment. As with acquaintance rape, an assertive student or employee may not be as easy to harass as a nonassertive person. In addition, as more and more people know how to assert their sexual rights, others may be more reluctant to intrude upon these rights.

5. *Reap other benefits, such as knowing what to say to influence what is happening in your society.* Or you may wonder how to handle unusual situations such as obscene phone calls or exposure to an exhibitionist—should you say anything to sex offenders you encounter?

Most of us have come from families who discouraged us from speaking up about precisely what we need or feel. Well-meaning parents could not possibly have foreseen how necessary sexual assertion would be to their children's welfare. They uᶜ ally were not taught assertion. They met fewer strangers; mutuaɩ trust and concern about reputation ensured their sexual safety in most situations. Society depended upon the good manners of each person and rewarded humility and reticence; children learned to avoid a "big head" or a "smart mouth." Those who misused their power by harassment, abuse, or rape were not, as a rule, discovered or discussed. Like my great-grandmother, the victims were powerless.

No one likes a pushy person. You would not want to become so intent on your own rights that you become rude or trample on the rights of others. One reason more people are not able to assert themselves is positive, in a sense: they are trying to avoid angry or rude outbursts and are afraid their anger will get out of control. Not knowing any halfway point between nonassertiveness and aggression, they keep quiet. Their assumption is that if you are not passive, you are aggressive.

WHAT IS SEXUAL ASSERTIVENESS?

Assertion, or assertiveness, is behavior in which you stand up for your rights and say directly what you believe, want, and feel. Assertive people do this appropriately and honestly while respecting other people's rights as well. The assertive person speaks up in her own defense, but does so without any effort to harm or put down another person.

Let's listen to Susan, who has been out with John several times. She's worried about sexually transmitted diseases, and their relationship has been getting more passionate. One night, after some kissing and petting that they both enjoyed, she decides to bring up her concerns.

> *Susan:* (Pushes John back and looks at him) John.
>   (Sighs). I need to stop for a minute. I need to talk.
> *John:* What for?
> *Susan:* Things are going pretty fast here, and I'm...just
>   worried about going too fast.
> *John:* What's to worry about if you feel good? (He tries
>   to kiss her on the neck.) Come on, Sue.
> *Susan:* (Leans back a bit) John, you know I like you and
>   I'm very attracted to you, but (she takes a deep
>   breath) I think we need to talk about...protection...
>   before we go any further.

Susan sticks to the point of what she needs. She expresses her views without putting John down. Since John was not out of line in merely wanting to continue enjoying what they were doing, she does not get angry.

Aggression, on the other hand, is behavior aimed at hurting or dominating. For example, consider Al and Linda. They've been out a few times, and Al has asked Linda to spend the night at his place.

> *Al:* I wish you would, Linda. You know how much I
>   want to be with you.
> *Linda:* Cut it out, Al! You men are all the same!

Linda's response is aggressive. She lashes out at Al and labels him and all men. She might really prefer that her outburst not escalate into bad feelings between them. She would rather have spared his feelings, since he was just asking for—not forcing—what he wanted. But she wanted to postpone further sex and she didn't know how to be assertive. An assertive response would have been:

> *Linda:* I know you want to, Al. But I'm just not ready for
>   that yet.

Here she showed she was sensitive to his feelings, but she made it clear what she wanted.

In a *nonassertive* response a person does not stand up for his or her own wants and needs. This behavior usually comes from feeling helpless and threatened. An example is Kathy and Jim, who are sitting in the car, kissing. Kathy starts to unbuckle Jim's belt. Jim takes her hand away.

> *Kathy:* Come on, Jim. You know I want you.
>
> *Jim:* Oh, Kathy, I don't know, I just...I don't think we should.
>
> *Kathy:* Just stay out here a little longer.
>
> *Jim:* But, Kathy...you know, you really turn me on, you know you do...but we just met last week and...
>
> *Kathy:* What kind of man are you? Am I ugly or something?
>
> *Jim:* No, you're not. (She gives him a very long kiss. He's aroused and thinking he should prove his manhood. After awhile they go inside and have intercourse, without a condom.)

Jim did not stand up for his rights. Although he was feeling passionate, he also was worried because he knew he was endangering himself as long as he did not talk over sexual protection with Kathy. He allowed sex to progress to the point where it was too late to discuss risk. And of course, as sexual attraction distorts his judgment, Kathy seems more and more wonderful and problem-free. But he's known her only a week and could not possibly have enough information to justify taking a sexual risk with her.

Books about assertiveness training always give scenarios about what people *say* when they're not being assertive. But many nonassertive sexual situations involve few, if any, words! If any words were spoken, the typical nonassertive scenario would go like this:

> *A:* God!
>
> *B:* (Kisses A, rubs body against A)
>
> *A:* (Pulls B closer, then pulls away)
>
> *B:* What? (Kisses A's neck)
>
> *A:* No, I...
>
> *B:* Please, just...
>
> *A:* I—I—(lies down on car seat, pulling B down on top)

Assertiveness training has become popular all over the country as a way to help Americans learn how to speak up for themselves in a nondefensive, rational way most likely to solve problems. Classes in assertiveness training abound in colleges and other adult education courses. Students are trained to be assertive but not aggressive. Yet in very few of these books or classes is sex ever mentioned! It is really "All-but-sexual" assertiveness training. Few teachers want to tackle as controversial and emotional a subject as sex and many audiences are self-conscious hearing about it. Partly because we avoid crude or distasteful sexual remarks in the interest of being well-mannered and polite, we make the entire subject taboo. Many professionals feel embarrassed to treat the subject with their students or clients because they themselves are not at ease discussing such matters. Studies of physicians indicate a widespread inability to discuss sex with their patients.

In a "polite society," we implicitly agree not to discuss sexual matters. (If I say at a dinner party that I specialize in sexual assertion, an awkward silence follows.) Despite this great silence on the subject, I believe that sexual assertiveness is teachable. You may not be totally comfortable discussing sexual matters. That's "normal" in that most Americans feel such discomfort. But you deserve better.

Somehow while growing up I realized the absurdity of powerful adults—those people who knew all the answers—being reduced to embarrassed muteness by the mere mention of sex. I hope you, too, see the insanity of allowing a forbidden subject to threaten our society. Twenty years from now, our children will not thank us for saving them from hearing sexual words at the expense of their happiness and perhaps their lives.

THE THREE FACES OF ASSERTIVENESS

Patricia Jakubowski and Arthur Lange, two of the best known authors on the subject of assertiveness training, describe three kinds of assertion.[7] These apply very well to sexual situations.

The first kind of assertion is *empathic assertion*. In this case, the individual asserts himself by first acknowledging the other person's feelings—that is, showing sensitivity to the other person before asserting oneself.

For example, if Joe is being pressured verbally by Christie, he could be assertive and still empathic:

> *Christie:* (Pulls him to her, kisses him) Come on, Joe, please, what's holding us back?
>
> *Joe:* I know you'd like to make love, Christie, but I'm not ready for that.

Here Joe has stood up for his own feelings, but he has been sensitive to Christie and does not try to hurt her. He sticks to the subject of his own reactions.

The second kind is *escalating assertion*, in which the person begins with mildly expressing himself, but, because his partner does not listen or respond, the intensity of his statements escalates:

> *Christie:* Come on, Joe, you know you want me.
>
> *Joe:* I...I'm just not ready to go that fast. Let's be responsible, like they say.
>
> *Christie:* Come on, you know you need it. Joe, I just want you so much. (She tries to pull him toward her)
>
> *Joe:* I want you, too, but...not yet.
>
> *Christie:* What's your problem, hon? You got a problem with sex or something?
>
> *Joe:* I really get mad when you talk like that! I said I'm not ready, and I don't appreciate being put down.

Does it seem strange to hear the man defending his right to refuse sex? Men of all ages are going to need to acquire the skills to be able to do this—and soon—if they are to protect themselves.

The third kind of assertion is *confrontive assertion*. One confronts a partner when she *does* something that contradicts what she *says*. Suppose, for example, Bill tells his wife, Jean, that he would prefer that she not come on to him sexually after his evening run; he's very tired and can't respond as well until he showers first and rests awhile. Jean has repeatedly kissed him, touched him suggestively, and otherwise acted very seductively when he comes out of the shower. He feels embarrassed because he has had some sexual difficulties when he is tired, so he asks her to wait. She agrees. But now, two weeks later, she goes back to her old behavior:

> *Jean:* Mmmmmmmm...(she runs her hands over his chest). Want to lie down awhile?
>
> *Bill:* Jean! What's going on here? We talked about this and now here you go again. I'm really upset—don't you remember what we agreed?

Here Bill confronts Jean directly with the fact that she's not living up to what she said. He doesn't let her get by with it, but *he does not respond aggressively.* He sticks to the point.

This book is intended to help the reader think of ways to say whatever needs to be said about sex—directly, honestly, and appropriately. Every day, just by going to the movies or turning on the television, we can hear people saying things about sex that are devious, insulting, or manipulative. We have less experience seeing and hearing people discuss it in a healthy way.

VERBAL SELF-DEFENSE

We spend a lot of time and money in karate and other kinds of self-defense classes. In one sense, this book is about self-defense training. But it is about verbal, not physical, self-defense. The characters in the scenes are responding to the words or actions of others, but only with words. Assertive language might help to prevent someone's using physical force against you; it might even stop someone in the midst of using violence. But once force is being used, there is physical risk and other kinds of advice might be needed. Assertive responses are most effective when the person to whom you are speaking is capable of some rational thought. Please remember that this book refers only to prevention before physical force occurs. For sources of help against sexual violence, see the Appendix.

CHAPTER TWO

Understanding Assertiveness

I am not in this world to live up to your expectations,
and you are not in this world to live up to mine.[8]
—Fritz Perls

YOUR SEXUAL RIGHTS

Some people think they have no right to *ask* for what they want. Others feel they do not have a right to *refuse* except under certain circumstances, sometimes even in marriage. Some even believe that being made fun of in sexual ways at work, while slightly embarrassing, is something one just has to endure. We need to be able to understand, and to state explicitly, our sexual rights. Only then can we assert our power over our own bodies.

These fundamental rights to which I believe everyone is entitled are not legal rights, although some of them are built into our laws. You may want to add to this list with ideas of your own.

1. *A person has a right to refuse any type of sexual contact at any time or place, regardless of how aroused the partners might be.* There is no such thing as being so aroused that you "owe"

15

anything to your partner. If you are stark naked and change your mind, you still have a right to do so. Now, if you take off your clothes and change your mind on numerous occasions, you still have a *right* to do this, but there is an element of game-playing—and probably anger and manipulation—in it. Your body is still yours, though, and you are the only one who can make decisions about it.

Students in my classes role-play in order to learn how to resist sexual pressure. We set up four chairs and pretend that the "main couple" is alone together. The other two chairs are for "coaches" who help out when the main players get stuck. Our role-plays do not involve touching; the audience has to imagine that. First the man verbally pressures the woman. Then they reverse roles and the man refuses the woman's pressure. Men are sometimes willing to participate in the first situation, but when women pressure them, young men invariably react strongly. Indeed, only a few brave ones volunteer for this exercise. They show such signs of anxiety as repeating phrases. They often cop out; instead of resisting pressure, they make up a reason why they cannot have sex: "I have a girlfriend already." They sometimes sit down and refuse to play the role. Men are highly vulnerable in this society to the fear of appearing unmanly. Saying "Yes" has been ingrained in them as the only position a real man can take. ("Go for it!" "Score!") *This attitude must change*, or the rate of sexually transmitted disease (STD) will continue to increase at an alarming rate.

Going out with someone, buying dinner or doing other favors does not confer sexual rights to one person over another. This kind of misunderstanding, though, might be one good reason for women to start paying their own way or making the extent of their sexual availability clear before accepting gifts or favors. Unfortunately, some people feel they deserve something sexual for their money.

2. *A person has a right, in a sexual relationship, to express frustration and disappointment if sexual contact is refused.* If you refuse to continue sexual activity when both of you become very aroused, your partner has a right to express disappointment.

That is, other people have a right to their feelings, and you have a right to yours. However, a person who frequently asks for more sex and then expresses disappointment, even though the partner's position has been made clear, may be seen as a high-pressuring person. I once knew a young, beautiful woman who asked her husband to make love at least once a day. He felt so pressured that he began to balk during lovemaking. Finally he let her know that he felt pressured, even though she asked with a big smile. Their sex life improved.

3. *A person has a right to request any type of sexual activity in a sexual relationship, as long as it does not violate anyone else's rights.* The partner, however, has a right to decide whether to comply. If you've always wanted to try intercourse hanging from the chandelier, you can ask for it, but your partner has a right to think you're asking too much. You can ask for anything you want, but asking does not give you a right to receive it. If the partner should respond with horror or disgust, the "asker" must assess the effect of his or her request on their relationship. You also need to be sensitive to the culture in which you're living— certain requests will be perceived as insulting or even nauseating, despite being complimentary in another culture.

4. *A person has a right to any feeling, fantasy, or thought.* Whatever happens inside your head is yours. However, you are responsible for all of your behavior, which should not interfere with anyone else's rights. Normal people invent the most amazing fantasies and thoughts. Most of us would never dare share them with anyone else, for fear of being thought crazy or bad. Studies of fantasies reveal that far more people think about unusual sexual behaviors than actually do them.

Your right to any thought does not mean that your thoughts are all healthy for you or for others. If, for example, a person seems obsessed by certain thoughts, she may need professional help. If a married woman is constantly bothered by daring sexual thoughts about her daughter's husband, these thoughts might cause her to take actions that could endanger some of her family relationships. She might need the help of a counselor (see Appendix for resources). Or a person could be a "sexual addict" whose distorted thoughts trigger exhibitionism or child abuse. Most Americans have a religious background in the Judeo-Christian tradition, which has not always made clear the boundaries between thoughts and actions. In contrast with some religious doctrines, mental health professionals tend to ignore people's thoughts and fantasies unless they trigger harmful emotions or actions.

5. *Partners involved in a sexual relationship have a right to share expenses that in any way result from their sexual involvement.* Their mutual obligation includes sharing the cost of contraceptives and expenses resulting from pregnancy. Deception by one, however, might change the rights of the other.

6. *A person has a right to know if a potential sex partner has a contagious disease of any kind, or could possibly have been exposed to one.* Did previous lovers exhibit any of the symptoms of sexually transmitted disease listed on pp. 78–79. Had they engaged in any high-risk experiences such as sex with multiple partners, sex with people who frequent prostitutes, or with people who have shared intravenous drug needles? A couple entering a sexual act are taking certain chances, but each person has a right to hear whatever the other knows about the risk. You have a right to information and you should ask assertive questions. Your right to know, however, does not guarantee that your partner will tell the truth. Current research indicates that from one-third to one-half of sexually active people say they would lie to another person in order to get sex.[9] Trusting someone you do not know well with your body is simply not smart.

7. *A person planning sexual intercourse has a right to know whether the partner is using a contraceptive or other protective device, and any pertinent facts about it.* Condom users have a right to know whether the condom is latex (the most effective kind), whether it is new or five years old, and whether it is being used correctly. A man has a right to know whether his partner missed her pill any day that month.

8. *A person has a right to be free from becoming the object of unwanted sexual remarks or unwanted sexual gestures.* "Look at the knockers on that broad!" yelled down from a construction site, or a whistle from the street corner, is a form of intrusion, sex without consent. However, the one who sees a sexually attractive person has a right to feelings that do not result in offensive behavior.

9. *A person has a right to use the telephone without the intrusion of uninvited sexual remarks or sexual threats.* An obscene phone call is an expression of hostility, a violation of sexual privacy, and another form of sex without consent. It is also a crime. The overwhelming majority of women in the United States have experienced this form of sexual intrusion. We should be deeply concerned that the practice of anonymously frightening someone with sexual threats is so widespread.

10. *A person has a right to be free from physical contact of any kind unless he clearly indicates a desire for it.* Between strangers, this prohibition is very clear. Touching another person's buttocks, breasts, or genitals without consent, for example, is illegal in most states. And the consensus that exists in our society which forbids more extreme force, such as rape, is rarely a point of disagreement. However, some acquaintance rapists claim that they misunderstood the women's intentions. He may believe that her "No" means "Yes." Novels, television and films, and songs in our society encourage that view.

11. *A person has a right in a relationship with a helping professional (such as a doctor, psychologist, attorney, psychiatrist, member of the clergy, or teacher) to be free from any sexual suggestions, advances, or pressures.* The needy person seeking help is particularly vulnerable to the rationalizations and whims of those in positions of power and status. Such an unequal relationship is based on trust. The codes of ethics of most helping professionals prohibit any sexual contact or dating, and they are well aware of the ethical implications. Many believe that a therapist who has intercourse with a patient should be charged with rape.

12. *A person has a right to work at his/her place of employment free from sexual communication or solicitation of sexual contact of any nature, when submission to or rejection of such contact is intended to impose favorable or adverse working conditions.* That cumbersome statement is the wording of the federal statute that protects

men and women from sexual harassment, which ranges from undesired sexual remarks to the actual firing of an employee for resisting sexual overtures. (If some heterosexual readers cannot imagine men being threatened by a sexual offer, only imagine yourself being propositioned by an employer who is extremely unattractive or whose sex is the same as yours.) On the job, employees should be judged only by job performance and not by the granting or refusing of sexual favors.

13. *A person has a right to wear the clothing of choice, providing it is within the law.* However, if others frequently react to your clothing with sexual remarks or arousal, you must confront the reality that these clothes are communicating a sexual message. If Tamara wears a T-shirt that says, "Make Me An Offer," she is within her rights, but she needs to know that it may provoke a sexual reaction. If Mary's blouse is transparent, she needs to anticipate its effect on other people. Despite their reactions, however, no one has a right to violate Mary's or Tamara's sexual rights. Until informed otherwise, those who see through Mary's blouse or read Tamara's shirt should assume that clothing styles are not requests for sexual activity. Of course, some employers require uniforms; employees occasionally have protested the requirement to wear a revealing or seductive uniform in the workplace.

14. *A child has a right to be protected from any contact or experience with an adult which is for the purpose of that adult's sexual arousal or satisfaction.* This restraint goes beyond the types of sexual contact that are illegal, such as rape or molestation. It also includes words or gestures that the adult finds arousing. Children are amazingly sensitive; they know when they are being exploited.

15. *A child has a right to know what will happen to his or her body at puberty and the implications of those changes.* At present only twelve states require sex education in the schools. Some school districts have actually passed down directives that the words "intercourse" and "condom" are not to be mentioned in school. Yet research indicates that very thorough sex education reduces the rate of disease and pregnancy.

Should the following also be a right, or is it just a desirable situation that one can hardly expect?

16. *A person has a right to know the intentions of a partner before they have sexual intercourse.* If it means strictly recreation to one partner, and love to the other, does each partner have a right to know about these feelings? Or is it merely important information—be careful, but you must take your chances, since love cannot be guaranteed?

You may have thought of rights that you could add to this list, or revisions you would want to make. But the major point is that there *are* certain "givens" for fair-minded people.

Thinking about these rights and integrating them is very important to your ability to be sexually assertive. If you do not believe you have sexual rights, your actions will reflect your fears and uncertainties. Any efforts you make to protect yourself would lack real conviction; even if the other person is unaware of what is causing it, confusion will result.

BODY LANGUAGE

You convince another person that you really mean what you say not only with words, but, sometimes unconsciously, with gesture and posture. You might be able to say assertive words, but unless your body conveys your sincerity, they will sound canned and false. Your body shows your intent to stand up for your rights. Most people generally can look someone right in the eye, most of the time. If you are assertive you generally hold up your head rather than hang it down sheepishly. Your voice is not timid and uncertain, but strong enough to show that you mean what you say.

But when you're discussing difficult sexual topics—especially if you're sexually aroused—it's natural to hem and haw a bit at first. You should congratulate yourself on even beginning to open up these important subjects. The more you realize you have the rights described above, the more your total appearance and voice convey that you really mean what you say.

There may be some mixed messages when you say what you want sexually. You may say what you *think* is best for you after you've just been kissing or petting passionately with someone. It should be understood that, if you are doing this, you are usually attracted to the person and *part* of you wants to go further. Or, to put it another way, your higher brain has considered intercourse and decided to refuse it, while other parts of your brain and body are trying to propel you forward into delightful passion. A person rarely enters a situation which increases an appetite that he decides to postpone. Going on a diet is similar to restraining sexual desire: you deny yourself some satisfaction for a "higher" reason—health or appearance. You could hardly expect a dieter who is hungry to act as if she were not, but neither would you try to force food upon her.

So you need to decide what you're communicating to the other person if you say you don't want intercourse but your body language conveys the opposite. It's probably best if you explain how far you want to go so that the other person doesn't think you are protesting without meaning it:

> "I love to kiss but I don't want to go any further."

> "It's important to me to keep my clothes on—that's sort of my boundary line."

> "I need to let you know how far I want to go, because I'm so attracted to you, you may not realize that I..."

If It Ain't Broke Don't Fix It. Talking about sex may be easier than you think. Not everything you want to say requires expert advice. Recently I asked students to submit questions they had about sexual communication. One student wrote, "How do I tell a nurse I've been hit in the genitals with a baseball?" This illustrates the common fallacy that experts necessarily know better than we do. I told him to tell the nurse, "I've been hit in the genitals with a baseball."

I-STATEMENTS

If you need something or are asserting your right to something, it is best to speak clearly and straightforwardly.

The simplest tool for doing that is called the "I-statement," which includes your emotional reaction. These expressions not only say what you think, but they also stress how you feel. Tony and Joan, for example, have been married for ten years. Sometimes Joan reads books about improving sex in marriage. Often she tells Tony about the books in great detail. He feels threatened because he's afraid she's hinting that he needs to be a better lover. After she's brought up the subject several times, he decides to be open about it:

> *Joan:* Look, Tony, here it says some people have sex in ten different positions!
>
> *Tony:* You know, I feel really uncomfortable when you tell me all those things you read about. (He decides to make another I-statement.) I'm a little worried that you will expect too much from me.

Here Tony takes responsibility for his own reactions in an assertive manner. He labels what he feels. He does not blame himself or Joan.

It may seem like a big risk to lay your feelings open in this way. It makes you vulnerable. But if you *can't* say how you feel, you are a lot more vulnerable to things that will happen *later* if you don't speak up.

One of the biggest mistakes in sexual communication is the You-statement, which usually blames the other person. It puts him on the defensive and is usually aggressive. How would this scene above have gone if Tony had made a You-statement?

> *Joan:* Look at all these suggestions for better sex, Tony.
>
> *Tony:* You always bring up those damned books! You never just let things happen naturally!

Is Joan more likely to see Tony's viewpoint after this? Probably not. When people accuse and blame us, we're likely to go straight into defending ourselves. But after hearing a partner's statement of his own feelings, we have a chance to stop and think about his reaction to what we are doing.

Here's a comparison of some important sexual communications contrasting I- and You-statements:

I-STATEMENT	**YOU-STATEMENT**
I need more time.	You're always rushing me.
I'm embarrassed...	You shouldn't say that (or do that).
I'm scared.	You're scaring me.
I'm disappointed.	You let me down again.
I'm not ready for that.	You are too pushy.
I need to talk about our lovemaking.	You keep putting me off.
I'm not comfortable having sex without a condom.	You aren't considering my feelings about condoms.
I don't feel aroused.	You're not turning me on.

You can learn a little "starter" phrase to get yourself going in order to make an I-statement. First, think of what you really *feel*. You're experiencing some emotion, like pride, thrill, anger, irritation, guilt, jealousy, embarrassment, disappointment, fear, or discomfort. Then plug the emotion into one of these sentences:

> *"I feel _____ when you do that."*
> Or:
> *"I'm _____"* (mentioning the feeling).

This technique may seem canned and artificial at first, but you'll get used to it so that you can fit I-statements into your conversations more easily.

"I'm uncomfortable" is my favorite all-purpose statement of feeling. It can be used in many situations without having to give reasons. You can say you're uncomfortable when you can't pinpoint your exact feelings, but you feel a need to speak up anyway:

A: Remaining a virgin is important to me.

B: Why?

A: It just is.

B: You must have some reason.

A: It's what I've decided.

B: But why? Sex is good for you. You need it.

A: Look, I'm uncomfortable with all this pressure.

Practice making such statements about small issues. They can help you in nonsexual situations, even with your family:

I'd like some help with this.

I'm so proud of you.

I'm disappointed that you were late.

These expressions are not magic, of course. They are simply an improvement over most people's communication. In the area of sex, they are usually a vast improvement. For the best outcome, however, you need a willing listener who has some concern about your feelings. In other situations, like the above conversation about virginity, you may still want to state your position clearly even if the other person is not a good listener. I-statements *increase your odds* of getting your feelings across successfully to another person. That's what this book is really about—increasing your odds of protection by sexual assertiveness.

STAYING SOBER

Sexual assertiveness depends on higher brain functions. That means that you need to have a clear head so you can think about the consequences of your behavior and defend yourself if necessary with words or actions. You cannot think clearly under the influence of a mood-altering chemical such as alcohol, cocaine, or marijuana. *The overwhelming majority of young women who become pregnant unintentionally, contract a sexually transmitted disease, or are raped by an acquaintance, are intoxicated at the time.* Men can be raped—usually by a male—and drug use increases the odds of this kind of victimization. As many as three-quarters of sex offenders, particularly rapists, had been drinking at the time of their crime. Even a couple of drinks can lower your inhibitions against doing things that are self-destructive.

Many readers of this book will be untreated chemical dependents, or care about someone who is. Please, inform yourselves by calling the National Council on Alcohol and Drug Abuse or other numbers listed in the Appendix. Then attend meetings and find out where to start on the road to sobriety. There is more help now than ever before.

USING YOUR OWN WORDS

In the following pages I will suggest many ways to talk about sex. It is best for you to take what you like and rephrase it in your own words. Getting across your *meaning* is what counts.

CHAPTER THREE

Taking Charge of Your Thoughts

There are certain "silent assumptions"
that probably still lurk in your mind.[10]
—David D. Burns

"I can't help it, I can't help myself."

So ran Ray's thoughts as he decided to have unprotected intercourse with the third partner that week. But nobody forced him to take that risk. In actuality, Ray made a choice. Thousands of people protect themselves sexually, and they feel just as passionate as Ray did. But there is a crucial difference between Ray and those people: what they *believe.* Ray believed he was helpless against his sexual impulses, so he did not try to protect himself or his partner.

Because she *believed* it was unromantic to mention birth control, Jackie became pregnant. She is not unusual; in fact, even teens who have been sexually active for some time tend to use either unreliable methods or no birth control at all. Why? Because they believe they cannot get pregnant, or they feel it is unromantic, or they think that women should not be assertive.

The things you believe are the among the most powerful influences in your life. And of all the things that influence you, your beliefs are among those over which you can gain control.

The decisions people make depend upon what they believe. They are usually unaware of how their beliefs guide them, but these assumptions lie there in the background at every moment. If you strongly believe something, it's all you can do to keep that attitude to yourself. Can you pick out what Paul believes?

> *Angela:* You're lucky I'm dating you—probably not many women would go with a guy who has your eye problem—I mean, your eyes look funny.
>
> *Paul:* (Looking miserable) I just know...I don't want to break up with you.

Paul has an eye problem that makes his eyes appear to be focusing on separate places. But why did Paul let Angela get by with such an insulting remark? *Because he really believes nobody else would care about him.*

Your beliefs show—not only in what you *do*, but in your tone of voice, your facial expressions, even the pauses in your conversation. Even if you try to put on an act, it will have very little impact. It might even confuse the other person.

Your sexual beliefs—about your rights, your ethics, your pleasures—are a commanding energy in guiding your actions. And a variety of outside sources influence your sexual beliefs.

CULTURAL MESSAGES

Our society sends hundreds of sexual messages. Some are positive. A major shift during the last fifty years, for example, has brought us to the belief that people deserve sexual pleasure. But often cultural messages confuse us and undermine sexual assertiveness. While these societal messages are rarely written down, they are definitely implied.

See whether you notice anything peculiar about the following remarks:

> *She:* Come on, Phil, what are you saving your virginity for?
>
> *He:* I'm just not ready. (He lowers his eyes shyly.)

Julie took him in her arms with the strength of months of waiting, and felt him slowly begin to respond.

Myrna was the most powerful woman in the company, and when Jack saw her pass his desk he secretly dreamed of the day when she would speak to him.

Did any of these comments "snag" you? They probably did, because each reverses our cultural messages that tell men and women how they are supposed to act.

Male Messages

Little boys pick up the message that they are supposed to be powerful, not act like a "sissy," and compete at all times ("score"). When a young woman pressures a young man, he believes he should stay in the "powerful" role. Everything in his society has taught him to believe this "fact." The powerful role has one major requirement in this situation: A powerful man must *conquer* a woman sexually, certainly not *submit* to any of her requests. So when a woman insists that a man use a condom, the man's fear of giving in may cause him to refuse. This is dangerous to his health, and to hers.

Female Messages

On the other hand, we do not encourage women to seek success and power, but instead to value love and relationships. Girls pick up the message that they are supposed to be nice and loving, and to wait until they are "chosen." So a woman may be scared of losing the love of a man if she shows power by insisting on sexual protection. In some minority communities, for example, it is unthinkable for a woman to insist on a man's doing anything—he loses machismo if he gives in. Women need to learn new skills in order to insist upon condoms and other sexual protection. But they also need to *believe* that they can be feminine and still have power over themselves.

Beliefs about male and female roles are just a few of the sexual beliefs stored there in your mind, guiding you all the time. But if you're going to protect yourself, you're going to have to think rationally, in an unclouded way. You can't act in your own interest if your beliefs are confusing you.

Take my student Jean for example. We were role-playing with Mark, who was doing a great job carrying out his instructions to be pushy. Jean seemed uncomfortable. Their conversation went like this:

> *Mark:* Come on, baby, come on, we'll use protection. I won't tell anyone.
>
> *Jean:* I just don't...I just can't.
>
> *Mark:* Come on, you said you would.
>
> *Jean:* I know I did, but I'm just...not ready.

Seeing that Jean looked so uncomfortable, I stepped in and "doubled" with her:

> *Powell:* I'm going to pretend I am another part of you and you correct me if I don't say what you feel. Okay?
>
> *Jean:* Okay.
>
> *Powell:* I feel very uncomfortable playing this role. Is that how I feel?
>
> *Jean:* Yes.
>
> *Powell:* I want to help myself, but...
>
> *Jean:* A woman just can't come out and...I mean—it may sound crazy, but if a woman just says, "no way," people are going to think she's...she's...*a bitch...or a prude, or something.*

And there we have it. That statement epitomizes a fear American women have of asserting themselves about sexual issues. It is a terrible conflict for a woman to think a man won't accept her if she shows strength. Yet strength is what any adult needs—to do a job successfully, to be a parent, and to remain steadfast through life's stresses.

If we pretend to be weaker than we are, we attract people who will never really get along with us. When you behave in a healthy, confident way, you attract a different kind of person. As psychologist Abraham Maslow is reputed to have said of women, "Alleycats attract tomcats, and lionesses attract lions."

MIND VERSUS BODY

Sex is one of the few areas in life in which you might really feel like doing something with your *body* that your *mind* knows is not good for you. Cravings for alcohol and unhealthy foods, as well as compulsive exercising, are probably the only drives that compare at all to the sexual situation. You want your passionate feelings to happen in the right time and place, but what do you need to *believe* in order to be convincing when you assert your sexual rights?

FAMILY SCRIPTS

The Transactional Analysis people, Eric Berne and Thomas Harris, say that you are "scripted" in childhood for what you will do and say as an adult.[11] A life script is an early, unconscious program for what you will do with your life. As you grow, you learn how things do happen, and after a while you quite naturally assume that's how things are *supposed* to happen. You have been given internal beliefs, a "script" that you tend to act out; you go through life acting as you were taught to act, anticipating what you've been taught to expect. For example, you could probably write the rest of this scene from your own past experience:

> *You* (as a little kid): Mom, where do babies come from?
>
> *Mom:* I'll tell you later.
>
> Or:
>
> *You:* Dad, what's a condom?
>
> *Dad:* You're too young to be talking about things like that (or fill in what *your* dad would have said).

If your parents were uncomfortable, you probably stopped asking. They might have been willing to hang in there anyway, but hearing their discomfort you still were *scripted*: "Don't talk about sex."

You were also scripted either to stand up for yourself or to give in. An obedient child is a pleasure. Rebellion is annoying if not infuriating, so most of us learned to squelch some of our own feelings in order to obey adults. We say you were "scripted"—to obey without question, or to reason with others who disagree, to please everyone whenever possible, or to be devious. Whether you are fifteen or fifty, you remember the scripts of your childhood.

Joyce, for example, always tries to manipulate men by playing games with them. She believes in playing hard to get, but she also makes them think she likes them and enjoys pulling the rug out from under them periodically by dating someone else. Her mother manipulated her father all through Joyce's childhood, and Joyce watched and learned. Her mother even went so far as to advise her, "Never let a man know what you're thinking—keep the upper hand." Thus Joyce was scripted to manipulate men.

Don watched his dad and uncles drink. He heard his mother and aunts complain about it but saw that they did nothing. He was scripted to "Stay drunk and be out of control," and he lived up to it when he reached his twenties. This way of life affected his love-making and also gave him an excuse to impose sex on his dates.

We were also scripted about pleasure. Some of us got the message "Have fun!" and some of us got the message "Fun is risky." Even if they were unsaid, very clear messages in our families taught us whether to enjoy ourselves sexually when we became adults. A parent tries to hold back a child's interest in sexual activity by minimizing any talk about sexual pleasure. This is an effort to protect. But sometimes parents go overboard with warnings. No parent, even with the best intentions, can definitely give his child a positive script about sex. At first a child needs protection, but when he grows up he will need to view sex as a pleasure. So he may receive a confusing message: "Enjoy sex, but don't."

Some other sexual messages are these:

"You'll turn out to be a whore just like your aunt."

"I hope you'll sow your wild oats as I always wanted to."

"Your body is important—take care of it and enjoy it."

No one needs to have said the words to you directly—you got the message. And the message may have stayed with you the rest of your life. Up until now.

BELIEFS YOU WILL NEED

When your belief conflicts with what you are supposed to do, what you *believe* often wins. For example, if you really believe it's okay to make a mistake you can probably speak with ease in front of a group. But if you believe mistakes are terrible, you probably will not volunteer for any talking that would open you up to criticism.

If you are assertive you just naturally have a set of healthy beliefs. In a sense, you actually tell yourself healthy things—you have a running dialogue with yourself.

For example, someone gets in front of you as you are waiting in line. "He's not supposed to do that, it isn't fair!" says a part of yourself. And this inner voice may spur you to take action.

Or you're preparing for a date with a new person and you're scared you will get sexual too quickly as you have in the past. "Hope I can be careful," you say to yourself. And on another level you're probably saying: "I can't wait to touch him." Your passionate feelings tell you to do one thing, and your higher brain, capable of looking at long-range consequences, tells you to do another.

Or you're a male scripted to "Score!" A woman is an object to conquer. You may hear yourself thinking, "What could I do to get her to go all the way?"

Usually we aren't even aware of them, but certain situations bring these beliefs to the conscious level of our thoughts. For example, you may believe, "It's embarrassing to talk about sex to my partner." You don't realize you believe this until there you are with her, intending to speak up, feeling awkward and unable to reach even the hemming and hawing stage. You're telling yourself how *awful* it is to talk about sex to your partner or you're telling yourself you'll *hurt her feelings*, or you'll look like a *fool*, or any number of things; and that all of those things are *mortifying*. Someone else, on the other hand, might believe it's okay to speak up, and have none of these painful emotions.

Albert Ellis, a psychologist who doesn't mince words, attacks clients' unhealthy beliefs in psychotherapy.[12] He says that, before we can stop ourselves from feeling painful emotions, we have to stop negative thoughts—because they *create* our negative emotions.

For example, let's say Matt is getting ready for a date. He's been intending to discuss safer sex practices with this woman for a few days, since desire has reached the risky stage. His thought processes go something like this:

> *(Looking in the mirror, shaving): God, I better tell her (he pictures or hears himself beginning to talk about safer sex or hears his voice saying it). She'll think I'm a wimp. I should (he imagines her face looking disapproving), but I can't. I can't stand to think about it. She doesn't have any diseases. (He turns on the radio.)*

What Matt is saying to himself is, "It's terrible and awful if I talk to my date about sexual protection. If I do, I'll be embarrassed and feel dumb, and men are supposed to be in control. She may be uncomfortable and the whole thing will be a terrible catastrophe." Telling himself these things causes Matt's heart to beat a little faster and his muscles to tense. He actually flinches a little as he shaves. A therapist in the Ellis tradition would probably train Matt to "catch himself" in these negative beliefs and self-talk. Such a therapist would train him to substitute a more rational thought, something like this:

> *It might be somewhat awkward to talk to a woman about sex at this stage. If she doesn't like what I say, I might feel uneasy for a short time. However, she might respond positively and appreciate my courage in speaking up. If she does not, I can survive a little discomfort in order to help us be sexually safe.*

Sexually assertive people believe in the sexual rights in Chapter 2. They might differ here or there on these rights, but they are generally clear. When they are in a sexual situation, they might not be thinking consciously about their rights, but they're aware of them at all times. This may not be true of you. You may be confused easily when another person provokes guilt in you or threatens you. But if you're clear on your sexual rights, you believe the following:

1. I never have to please another person sexually unless the idea truly appeals to me.

2. If anyone rejects me for my sexual beliefs or preferences, I can survive and very likely find another person.

3. I am not a child who needs an adult to help me survive; I am an adult and I can take care of myself even if I have to be alone for a while.

4. I am capable of speaking up when I see a sexual risk, or a chance to improve my sexual relationship.

If, deep down, you believe those things, you will feel calmer and more able to cope.

COMMON BELIEFS ABOUT SEX

How healthy are your sexual beliefs? You need all the insight you can get about your sexual attitudes. Mark the following true or false:

__I can't control my sex drive.

__Chastity is bad for me and I can't stand it.

__Truly liberated men (women) have sex whenever they want.

__A virgin has not really entered adulthood.

__Having sex is the only way to hang on to a prospective mate.

__If I refuse sex I'll lose the other person, and that's disastrous.

__If someone else gets mad at me when I refuse sex or ask for protection, it's awful and horrible if I don't do what they want.

__If my partner doesn't like something I say or do, it's a calamity and I should feel awful.

__If I am rejected because of my beliefs I'll never find another person to care about.

___If my partner puts me down because I refuse sex, it's a horrible humiliation that would not happen to a real man.

___If I stop when I'm very aroused, I can't stand it.

___Discussing safer sex is unromantic and/or naughty.

___It's unfeminine to insist on something with a man you care about; he'll love you less if you do.

___Everybody else has a great sex life but me.

___I can't exist without someone to love.

___I need sex to prove I am attractive.

___I need sex to prove I'm a "real" man.

___Sex is my most important need.

What was your score? All of the above beliefs are unhealthy. They aren't "the truth." They are just opinions that some people tell themselves. Learn to rephrase your negative statements. For example, let's say you tell yourself, "It's terrible and awful if my partner puts me down when I bring up the subject of sexually transmitted disease."

A healthier statement would be, "It would be very nice (pleasant, comfortable) if my partner responded the way I want. However, since life is not perfect, he may possibly try to persuade me to his way of thinking instead. While I might feel uncomfortable for a while, I can certainly stand it in order to keep myself healthy."

Try to evaluate your sexual beliefs. Go back to Chapter 2 and read the sexual rights again. Do you believe you have the sexual rights discussed?

BELIEFS ABOUT YOUR HEALTH

Experts have studied people to find out what beliefs cause them to take the best care of their health. Those who are most careful about preventing AIDS tend to believe the following:[13]

1. I am susceptible to AIDS.
2. AIDS is a severe disease.

3. AIDS is preventable.
4. I should take active care of my health.

People who don't believe all of these statements obviously aren't going to try as hard to prevent AIDS.

SELF-ESTEEM

"You got me all worked up, and you say *NO*?" says one man in my class role-plays. The other partner, a woman, is looking at him uncomfortably, and is momentarily speechless. At this point I often go up to the speechless partner and point to the top of her head.

"What happens next," I say, "depends entirely on what's going on in here."

That's right. Because if her self-concept and self-esteem are low, she is at risk. If you don't think you deserve something, you won't assert yourself to get it.

What is self-esteem? The phrase refers simply to how much you value yourself. In *Raising a Child Conservatively in a Sexually Permissive World*, Sol and Judith Gordon suggest that an individual with high levels of self-esteem:

- feels good about himself;
- harbors a basic sense of trust in the self and others;
- doesn't exploit anyone;
- gets along in the family;
- has a sense of humor, and not at others' expense;
- forms relationships that are mutually enhancing; and
- cares about other people's welfare.[14]

It's terribly unfair, but low self-esteem is correlated with a huge number of life problems, including being prejudiced and failing to help others in emergencies. It is also involved in all kinds of sexual difficulties, such as exhibitionism and obscene phone calling. People with low self-esteem may treat themselves with disrespect and are sometimes unable to resist persuasion.

Your first responsibility in this world is to take care of yourself. If you don't think you are worth it, you won't do a good job of it. The easiest way to feel you're worth taking care of is to have been raised by wonderful parents who loved you and set limits. They would have had no significant problems with self-esteem themselves. If you had no major childhood illnesses, learning disabilities, abuse, or other traumas, that helps your self-esteem as well. (Parents aren't responsible for everything.) Since these ideal parents and trauma-free childhoods have been denied to most of us, we have the job of improving our self-esteem on our own.

Sometimes life events just challenge us and we rise to the occasion. We cope with problems, and our self-esteem improves. We accomplish things or help someone, and our confidence rises. But sometimes we need professional help to get over the damage of the past. Consult the Appendix for sources of help to improve your self-esteem.

HOW TO REWARD YOURSELF

One of psychology's greatest wisdoms is that behavior that is rewarded tends to happen more often. You can apply that rather obvious truth to mental rewards. You can reward yourself. Here is how this might work:

> Steve has had some near-misses with sexually transmitted diseases. In college, he contracted gonorrhea, and it was slow in responding to treatment, but he finally tested out okay. He once got his girlfriend pregnant in high school and she had an abortion. He's begun to realize that he needs to deal with his sexuality differently.
>
> He's just begun dating Vicki, a very sexy-looking woman whom he finds terrifically attractive. She's making every attempt to get him to have intercourse, although it's only their third date. However, he knows nothing about her sexual past or her sexual opinions. She seems to have had numerous other sexual partners. And, he's afraid she will shame him or he will feel stupid if he turns her down. He

knows condoms aren't risk-free and isn't even ready for a condom mentally, but physically he's ready for intercourse.

So, maybe even shaking with passion, he says, "Hey, Vicki, you really turn me on. But I want to slow it down a little—I feel like we're on a roller coaster!"

Vicki replies, touching him suggestively, "Good! Let's take a ride!"

Steve gets up and pulls her up from the couch by the hands. He takes a deep breath. "Vicki, I—I want to take my time here, for you and me both. It's tough to do.... But...why don't we go to a movie or something?"

Vicki searches his face. She seems to see his determination. "Okay," she says.

After Steve walks off to the movies with Vicki he says to himself, "That was rough, but I did the smart thing."

Steve is using the disease-prevention technique of self-reward. Even if she had reacted by putting him down, he could still tell himself he did the right thing. Whenever you do something that is good for you, take the time to congratulate yourself. It raises your self-esteem. Your culture is not going to reward you for being sexually assertive, and if you are a male, your friends probably won't either.

Right after you do something sexually assertive, you could say something to yourself to remind and reinforce yourself:

> "Wow! That was tough, but I did refuse to take a risk, even if he (she) wasn't happy."
>
> "That was great, tonight I explained my opinions about getting sexually involved on a casual date."
>
> "It's been three months since I did anything risky."

Or just plain, "Good for me!"

You can even reward yourself out loud, letting the other person know:

> A: "I'm glad I told you how I feel. That was hard to do."
>
> B: "I'm glad, too."
>
> A: "I'm getting better at it."

Even if the other person doesn't agree, you can reward yourself for being sexually assertive:

> *A:* "I'm glad I told you how I feel."
>
> *B:* "Well, it sure ruined my evening."
>
> *A:* "I'm sorry you don't like what I said. But I've tried so hard to get the nerve to speak up. I really needed to tell you that because it's been worrying me."

We're very critical of conceit. We don't like anyone to be too uppity around us; we feel inadequate, perhaps. Yet, ironically, most of us spend our lives trying to gain more self-confidence! That puts us in a bind—we can't be humble and very confident at the same time. I think there's no real danger that people who gain confidence will become obnoxiously conceited. So, compliment yourself in any way you can when you're being assertive, and even ask some significant other person to help:

> *A:* Honey, you know I've been trying hard to tell you that I want to keep using protection every time we make love.
>
> *B:* Yeah, I know.
>
> *A:* When I mention the subject, you always look so serious. Would you try to give me a little encouragement?
>
> *B:* Sure, I'll try.

BRAVE MEN AND WOMEN

Thousands of messages tell little boys and adolescents what a man should be. The self-esteem of American males gets tied up quite early with power, conquest, and bravery. But men especially need to reconsider their definition of bravery. When a man speaks up to defend himself from sexual problems, he needs to congratulate himself. It is brave to speak up against what the culture is saying. It doesn't take courage just to copy some muscle-bound macho hero saying yes to every female who offers her body. The mass media give young males no models of honest, realistic sexual behavior. Didn't James Bond have sex without a second thought with scores of gorgeous women? Didn't just about every TV or film hero you've ever seen take every sexy woman up on her offer in less time than it takes to shake hands?

An adult in his thirties may feel secure and experienced enough to speak frankly about sex. But how should the frustrated teenage boy feel who takes a deep breath, and tells a girl he needs to get to know her better? Far from feeling unmanly, he should compliment himself:

"I'm strong. What a man!"

As for women, they are often afraid to take a sexual stand that could in any way be described as courageous. Succeeding chapters will explain skills to overcome this fear.

GUIDED IMAGERY

Fantasizing can serve not only as a substitute for something sexual you want to do, it can also be a rehearsal for what you are *planning* to do. That is, you're more likely to do something if you have imagined it beforehand; the images are a first step toward the reality.

Professionals advise that people rehearse mentally before engaging in any important new actions. Psychotherapists frequently help clients to learn new behaviors by helping them to imagine themselves doing them. Athletic trainers may help athletes mentally rehearse a game or a race. A speech teacher may ask students to see and listen to themselves giving the important presentation. This is called visualization or guided imagery.

You can use your sexual thoughts and fantasies to help yourself in the same way. Sex educators recommend that you practice healthy scripts rather than fantasizing unhealthy or risky scenes. Let's listen to Dr. Price, who is training her client, Bob, in guided imagery.

Bob is a student coming to the counseling department for help with his personal and school problems. But he has had some sexual troubles. He has had nonspecific urethritis, a sexually transmitted disease that bounced back and forth between him and his girlfriend for months. His girlfriend broke up with him, partly due to the disease and its problems. Bob, a good-looking guy, has had many offers from women around campus lately. He's had intercourse a few times without protection, and last week he thought he had the STD again. It turned out to be a false alarm, but Bob is scared. He realizes he's been doing a lot of fantasizing about "scoring," which in his group means drinking and having spontaneous sex. Dr. Price is trying to get him to try a new kind of fantasy. We see them in her office. Bob is relaxed in a chair, eyes closed. Dr. Price says,

> *You take a deep refreshing breath and relax deeply....It is Friday afternoon and you're getting ready to go out. You imagine what you're going to do tonight. You know there's a party down in Don's room....You look forward to getting together with your friends and meeting some new people....You imagine yourself arriving at the party....Don meets you at the door with a new woman....She's very attractive....You have a drink....Everyone seems to be having a second drink, and a third....You look at the bottle. You're aware that you'd like to be comfortable, you would have had another drink by now....But you decide to have a soda instead....Don tries to urge another drink on you....You say, "No, thanks, I'm fine." You take a deep breath and feel good about staying sober. You feel relaxed without another drink, and you take a moment to enjoy that little surprise....*

Dr. Price goes on to build up a fantasy where Bob adds his own images. He imagines himself meeting an attractive woman at the party; she is seductive, he wants to have sex with her. But he imagines himself either postponing getting sexually involved, dating her, talking over any sexual plans they might have; or at least using a condom in any sexual contact that they have.

It's fun to have sexual fantasies before a date or sexual encounter, and it might help you to observe how you fantasize. You need only a few moments to include safer sex practices in your fantasies. There is research to show that people who substitute safer-sex fantasies have a lower rate of sexually transmitted disease than people who continue daydreaming about risky sex.[15]

THOUGHT-STOPPING

Most of us have been bothered by some of our thoughts at times. Maybe they weren't even sexual. Maybe you made a mistake and later said to yourself, "How stupid, how stupid!" You wanted to stop calling yourself stupid, but the thought kept popping into your mind. Or maybe you went over and over the mistake in your thoughts and felt the embarrassment or humiliation all over again.

Modern psychologists have come up with some clever and simple ways to change your thoughts. Hang on, because this is going to sound far-fetched. But evidence indicates that people can decrease or completely eliminate negative thoughts by yelling at themselves.

Either that or snapping a rubber band.

Yes, it is true. These are ways you can punish away an undesired thought. It's done like this: every time you have a negative thought, you yell, "Stop!" Yell out loud if you're alone or yell inside your head if you're with others. (Even your dog may not appreciate a sudden shock.) That means you yell *every time* you catch yourself having the undesirable thought.

Now, if you prefer another of these "punishment techniques," instead of yelling you may put a rubber band on your wrist and snap it hard every time you think an undesirable thought. I'm not worried about this technique sweeping the country, but it's actually proven quite an effective aid for treating certain habits.

Take Elaine, for example. Elaine engages in compulsive sex. She has had more partners than she can keep track of. She has already had two abortions and a case of chlamydia, and she knows that in the nineties her behavior could get her into even worse sexual trouble. After going to a therapist about this problem, Elaine realizes that she fantasizes a lot about picking up a stranger and having unprotected sexual intercourse. Her therapist is helping her catch herself in this fantasy, which is really a "rehearsal" of destructive sexual behaviors. Now, whenever Elaine catches herself in this fantasy, she snaps a rubber band against her wrist and substitutes a safer fantasy.

Or take Lavonne, who has been trying to get up the nerve to discuss condoms with her partner. Whenever Lavonne even *thinks* about the condom conversation, she says to herself, "He's going to get so mad!" Rationally, she knows that she must protect herself by discussing condoms. So every time she catches herself thinking of his anger, she yells, "No!" to herself. Gradually, the thought diminishes.

Every time you banish the undesirable thought, you should make yourself substitute a healthy one. After Lavonne yells,"No!" inside her head, she immediately says, "I'm helping us both. I'm doing him a favor, too." When she imagines sex with him, she imagines it *only* with a condom. This makes it easier to talk to her partner about using one.

THE PARTS OF YOU

There is another insight that can help some people to feel more secure. To learn this you'll need a little background.

We all have various "parts" in our personalities. This does not mean we have multiple personalities like the famous Sybil or Eve. Because normally, unlike Eve, we know about the different parts. For example, on many Friday afternoons part of you says, "Finish your work," and another part says, "Let's get out of here and enjoy." If you're kissing someone passionately, one part very likely says, "Where is the nearest private place where we can do whatever we want?" And another part (even if it seems like a weak little voice) may be saying, "I should..." (fill in the blank with the rational statements of your mind).

The various voices in us develop in childhood. Millions of people have grown up feeling both unloved and unsafe due to physically or emotionally scary things that happened to them. For example, Jerry grew up with a passive father and a controlling, seductive mother. While she did not actually touch Jerry in a seductive way, during his adolescence she often invited him in to talk to her as she put on her makeup, naked from the waist up. She told him lovingly that, when he was born, his aunts looked at him nude and said he would make some woman very happy someday. She mentioned wistfully times when he was nude as a child. She told him his father was sexually inadequate. She was jealous of his girlfriends.

During this time, his father was cold and hostile to Jerry. He had nowhere to turn. His father hated him, and his mother cared in a controlling, seductive way. His childhood was painful and lonely. He struggled with the confusing ideas about sex and love that he learned growing up. As an adult, he suffered from the most acute feelings of loneliness and pain.

When scary or hurtful things happen to a little child, these events can cause the person to become partly "stuck" in childhood. That is, feelings of fear, anger, or hurt felt in childhood keep coming up in adulthood *with the same intensity that the helpless child felt back then.* Even though it's not appropriate for an adult to feel so scared, helpless, or abandoned, she still retains the "child," with all the child's strong and painful feelings. We might say, in the words of the Transactional Analysts, the individual is operating in her "Child" at such times. She is bypassing the more adult and nurturant parts of herself because they weren't there when she was little.

You can see how the child part took over in the life of Mitch, who was compulsively sexual. He engaged in sex at virtually every opportunity. He knew it was risky in the nineties, and he even knew some friends who had been infected with STDs. But he desperately wanted to be loved. He grew up with very critical, rejecting parents. His father was an alcoholic who beat him. Whenever he got into a sexual situation that could involve risk, he felt helpless and little, as if he had to do whatever his partner wanted so he wouldn't relive those old feelings. After years of sexual troubles, he decided to take responsibility for those things and consult a professional for help.

After Mitch went into therapy, he began to understand his sexual compulsions. Whenever he was out with someone, just at the critical moment of deciding to go further sexually, he began to be aware of scary, awful feelings. He felt that he *had* to go ahead and have sex, regardless of safety or any other consideration. What he learned in therapy was, "I'm not little. I'm not stuck with two unloving parents anymore. I have a grown-up part of myself now that can take care of me and help me find love and avoid pain. That caring part of me is right there when I'm making sexual decisions, if I can just listen to it."

We all have a little child element incorporated in our personalities. For the lucky few, that aspect grew up so secure that as adults they never get those helpless childhood feelings of rage, desertion, shame, or terror. But for many others, stressful experiences trigger the little kid's old, painful feelings, necessitating reassurance.

On the other hand, we all have a grown-up part that we lacked in childhood. We all are more capable of protecting ourselves than that helpless child was, but sometimes we don't realize it. Adults' unawareness of their own power can cause them to feel

- totally alone with the feelings of an abandoned child rather than the temporary loneliness of an adult.
- as scared as if they might die, when they are really adult enough to stay safe.
- angry enough to kill someone, and afraid they have no control over their anger.
- terrified when someone else is angry at them, as if they were to be killed, rather than only a bit anxious as a secure adult might be.

Past feelings can influence your sex life. These strong feelings can encourage hasty sexual decisions. If you are not keeping yourself safe sexually, if you repeatedly take sexual risks or cause yourself other sexual problems—you may want to check out your thoughts and feelings. Could it be that, just when you're on the verge of deciding to go further sexually, you have the strong emotions you had as a child?

- I'm scared to back out now or he'll be mad and that's awful and terrible.
- At last someone loves me—I'll do whatever he says.
- If I just please her, I'll finally be loved.

Learning to get past your childhood fears can be an important step toward protecting yourself sexually. If you think your fears are causing you to make unwise decisions, you may want to find some professional help. (See Appendix.)

FEELING DOWN

Sometimes your mood puts you at risk for doing something sexually unwise. When you are depressed, you need to be extra protective of yourself, because you may be more vulnerable to sexual mistakes at such times.

A component of normal adults' personalities can watch out for them when they're depressed. Adults don't need a parent to take care of them anymore, but they do need to develop a "parent" within themselves.

When you're lonely or depressed, you need to be wary of the little tricks your mind can play on you. Because at such times the childlike irrationality in you may want sex for reassurance, regardless of your age.

You could talk to yourself when you catch yourself really down and say, "Self, I need to watch it here; I feel really defenseless. If someone should get sexually involved with me right now, I might be putty in her hands. I need to take special care of myself right now."

It's as if you were carrying something very delicate down the stairs. You might have bounded up and down the stairs when your hands were empty. But when you're carrying a valuable china dish, you watch your step, and remind yourself that you're carrying precious cargo. When you're feeling depressed, look out for yourself. You are precious cargo.

Donna's experience shows how mood and self-esteem affect sexual decisions. She is divorced, but, even though she was once married, she's never been close to a man. Her father left when she was nine and doesn't contact her. Donna is flirtatious and enjoys fixing herself up, going out, and meeting men. She dated a new man every couple of weeks and almost always had intercourse with him. After about four years of this behavior, she began to become alarmed about the kind of men with whom she was sleeping. She admitted to her friends that sex was like a hug to her—she didn't need sex as much as human touch. "I felt so alone in this world," she said. "I couldn't tell the difference between sex and love. It was a warm body to be close to."

Donna realized that not only was sex not helping, in this case it was putting her at risk for other serious consequences. Getting sex is not the same as getting love. Next time you think you want sex, take a deep breath and pause for a moment. Ask yourself, "If someone held me and hugged me, would I feel mostly satisfied? What else could I do to take care of myself right now?" Try to make sure what you want before you decide that sex is what you need.

SELF-HYPNOSIS

There are entertainers (stage hypnotists), and there are competent, well-trained professionals who use clinical hypnosis.

Some of their clinical methods guide people in behavior changes, such as control of overeating and smoking. Put simply, hypnosis can change your behaviors and thoughts by getting through on a very deep level of which you are usually unaware.

It is possible to help strengthen yourself with some of the self-hypnotic techniques used by clinical hypnosis. You need not perform any self-induction into hypnosis to borrow a few of their techniques. So as to concentrate fully, you should close your eyes and use these methods when you're not driving or doing anything else that requires your attention.

For example, Spiegel and Spiegel are psychiatrists who have helped numerous people quit smoking. They designed a kind of self-statement for smokers that can be helpful in changing sexual behavior. For smokers, it went like this:

> *Smoking is a poison to my body.*
>
> *I need my body to live.*
>
> *I owe my body respect and protection.*[16]

To use this technique with sexual behavior, you have to rephrase it to fit your situation.

Suppose, for example, that Rick engages in casual sex whenever he feels like it. Maybe he's an attractive person who can find numerous partners. He's worried because he has had curable STDs and knows he could become infected with the incurable ones.

He needs a reminder, to program his unconscious a bit by keeping healthy, self-protective thoughts foremost in his mind. So when he wakes up in the morning, and goes to sleep at night, and before he enters any situation that might tempt him to take risks, he closes his eyes, breathes slowly, and repeats to himself,

> *Casual sex is a risk to my body.*
>
> *I need my body to live.*
>
> *I owe my body respect and protection.*

Nina phrases her reminder a different way. She intends to keep having sex with a guy she is dating seriously. But she finds it easy just to forget about condoms, yet she knows her boyfriend has had many partners. She has had a couple of scares that she might be infected with an STD. After she had allowed herself to get swept away into unprotected intercourse, she felt depressed. She knows that even *curable* STDs might leave her sterile, and having children is very important to her future plans. She repeats to herself,

> *Unprotected sex is a danger to my body.*
>
> *I need my body to live and to have children.*
>
> *I owe my body respect and protection.*

This statement of her rational knowledge supports her and protects her from physical impulses. She stops, closes her eyes for a moment, and repeats her reminder to herself before she goes out with her boyfriend.

This technique is not for everyone. But some people enjoy developing their inner selves and using these kinds of mental strengtheners. People who compulsively take sexual risks may especially need frequent reminders of their inner strengths, just as an alcoholic may need to attend frequent AA meetings to keep strong ideas foremost in her mind.

THE HOLISTIC APPROACH

Research shows that frequent reminders have helped a number of people to avoid sexually transmitted diseases. Rather than try to help ourselves with just one technique or one viewpoint, it is better to bring in a variety of props and aids to healthy behavior. This is called the holistic approach. You can pick and choose from a number of ways to help yourself. One person may put reminders on the mirror or refrigerator:

YOU ARE STRONG

After all, how is anyone to know this statement means you are strong enough to drink less on a date, bring up the subject of condoms, or merely to have high self-esteem? You can attach little reminders here and there if you find them helpful. Even a symbol, such as a picture of yourself at a happy time, can be your private reminder.

A few people keep up the healthy reminders by joining groups that help them get past disturbing sexual messages. There are support groups, for example, for sexual addicts, incest survivors, and rape survivors. (See the Appendix for ways to find those groups.) Perhaps someday there will be groups where anyone needing support can talk about sexual concerns.

Whatever you choose to do, be aware that *your mind is already programmed sexually*. Your childhood has given you various sexual messages, and you have kept many of them throughout your teenage or adult life. Now you may want to add to those messages or try to change some of them to help yourself and any partner you might have.

II

HOW TO RESPOND TO PERSUASION

CHAPTER FOUR

Standing Up to Verbal Pressure

A time to embrace,
and a time to refrain from embracing.
—Ecclesiastes 3:5

Do all cultures have sexual pressure? Some wise scholar has pointed out that we can't really *know* about people's sexual activities in other societies. These faraway folks may not hanker to tell some visiting anthropologist what they do in private. But as far as we know, men have historically taken the role of the sexual "pursuer." Today women are encouraged to pursue men as well. In the nineties, just about anyone could find himself being sexually pressured.

Most societies do not promote getting sex by trickery or manipulation as much as we do in our media. "Wooing" someone with flowers, gifts, or compliments has been replaced in the media by the slick line. And the polite suitor has given way to the smooth operator.

THE CUSTOMS
OF SEXUAL PRESSURE

From the sixties through the eighties, the pill, abortion, and other technological changes allowed people to have sex without paying a high price. At the same time, we no longer agreed on strong standards or customs to fall back on as excuses to refuse sex. The following was a typical scenario in the fifties for a high school or college couple who had dated just a few times:

> *He:* (Puts his hand on her breast)
>
> *She:* (Likes it, but feels worried about her reputation, the prospect of intercourse, the possibility of pregnancy, her "marketability" as a marriage mate if she is promiscuous, his opinion of her)
>
> *She:* (Moving his hand away) No, I—I can't.
>
> *He:* Why not?
>
> *She:* I just can't, that's all.
>
> *He:* (Tries again more tentatively)
>
> *She:* Stop!
>
> *He:* I'm sorry.

A couple repeated this scenario, and perhaps progressed sexually, depending on how she felt about him. The use of force on a date, while it did happen, was not as common as it is today. He knew what her standards were likely to be; all "nice girls" had those standards.

The ideas that "nice girls don't" or "sex should wait until marriage" have now been openly questioned throughout our society. A woman on a date can't claim some strong belief in virginity based on the values of her family and community. She has to fend for herself and come up with her own reasons. More experienced women can rely on even fewer excuses. Many of the reasons women once used are no longer valid. "It will ruin my reputation"? Hardly a major concern in a society where sexual intercourse is taken for granted among most singles. While it was once considered the woman's responsibility to set sexual limits, now no one is quite certain whose role it is. Standards for men have not changed that much, and statistics show it. The greatest increase in premarital sex is among women. Most young men are still influenced by the standard that they should be out trying to "score," and now it has become an open competition about which many young men brag to each other. Because young males place such a high premium on sexual conquests, it is very difficult for them to turn down a sexual opportunity while still maintaining their composure and self-assurance. Men are "supposed" to

- pressure for sex when they can; and
- appear ready to accept just about any sexual offer.

This pressure to be a "stud" and prove one's masculinity changes the way sexual pressure occurs in our country. Listen to the words of one male college student describing what goes on between a man and a woman:

> A man is supposed to view a date with a woman as a premeditated scheme for getting the most sex out of her. Everything he does, he judges in terms of one criterion— "getting laid." He's supposed to constantly pressure her to see how far he can get. She is his adversary, his opponent in a battle, and he begins to view her as a prize, an object, not a person. While she's dreaming about love, he's thinking about how to conquer her.

Sexual pressure has become big business. Not just courting, but pushing, insisting, even getting rough. You see it in ads, in films and TV, and in songs. Look at how sexual pressure and violence are incorporated into song titles:[17]

"Leatherbound" Bitch

"She Likes It Rough" Trasher

"Screaming for a Love Bite" Accept

The lyrics of some of today's songs actually describe, in detail, how much fun it is to rape a woman. In order to resist sexual pressure, singles of any age need to learn how to recognize manipulation and sexual deception. They also need to learn how to give clear "yes" or "no" messages to a potential sex partner. In this chapter we'll talk about what you could say when someone tries to persuade you with words to go farther than you want to go. But this does not involve resisting physical force. It concerns only what you *say* to resist being verbally pressured into sex when you really don't want to.

USING YOUR HIGHER BRAIN POWER

Let us not underestimate the higher brain's ability to overpower the sex drive. Although nature's concern is with the human species, your own survival has a higher priority to you than survival of the human race. If the bear came over the mountain while your ancestors were becoming sexually aroused, their sexual responses stopped and they got out of there. Because of this safety feature, you have inherited the capacity to postpone or refuse sex. The turnoff mechanism was an advantage to survival.

In some societies, people still use great sexual restraint. Prior to the use of the birth control pill, people more commonly tried to postpone sex until marriage, and many succeeded. Of those who did not postpone, millions had fewer partners before marriage than unmarried people today, and fewer diseases.

BRAINWASHING

We've learned to think of sex as a process of being overwhelmed by intense passion without first thinking ahead. And we do have a capacity for the most delightful and delicious passionate feelings with no rational thought involved. It's wonderful to feel swept away, at least at that moment. But a kind of unintentional brainwashing also occurs in our society, which few of us criticize, in the hundreds of portrayals of people being carried away by passion.

Sex is the only appetite which we encourage one another to unleash. We don't accept dramas about ravenously hungry people who grab food and eat with no preliminaries. Some kind of preparatory behavior precedes eating, such as picking up a knife and fork, or asking someone to pass the food. But even in novels, the characters go straight to intercourse with no preliminaries. They never ask for a condom; unrestrained passion is the rule:

> I wanted him and he knew it and I knew he wanted me. But it was too soon, I hardly knew him...it couldn't be right...it...I was scared. "Chris...I..." "Shhh...everything's going to be okay." He wrapped his arms around me as we stood in the tall grass with our feet dug into the sand, and then I felt my body swaying with his, until we lay in the sand, and I was his. "Do you do this a lot, Chris?" The sun was still bright in the sky and we were still lying in his secret cove. "What? Screw?...Yeah...I do this a lot." "No, you smartass bastard. I mean like this. Here, in this cove. With someone you don't even know."[18]

The lovers in this popular novel never discuss the risk of disease or pregnancy. People who want to, have sex—of course! The fantasy of sexual freedom sells products, and it sells films, books, and movies. How do you protect yourself from sexual problems in the face of this kind of propaganda?

RECOGNIZING PRESSURE LINES

In the past few years I've polled my students about the best sexual pressure "lines" they've ever heard. I explain that a "line" is manipulative and dishonest, spoken by a person who is trying to get sex by devious means, whereas, if someone says the same thing sincerely, it is not manipulation. Younger and inexperienced people are usually the most prone to fall for these lines, but in the heat of passion or infatuation, even people in middle age can be vulnerable.

For example, "I love you" could be the best words you've ever heard, and part of a beautiful relationship. But if you're out with someone who has "been through" everyone in your group sexually, who's never shown any interest in you as a person, and who, necking passionately with you, says, "I love you"—*doubt it.*

Obviously the context in which someone makes a loving remark provides clues about whether it's true. But being "in lust" or "in love" leaves you open to believing statements that look humorous on the printed page.

Over the years, my surveys have come up with a long list of lines, most of which fall into definite patterns:

Lines That Declare Love and Caring

"I don't want to have sex with you—I want to *make love* to you."

Lines That Reassure You about the Negative Consequences

"Don't worry, I'm sterile."

"You can't get pregnant the first time." (This is not true.)

"Don't worry—I'll pull out." (Withdrawal before ejaculation will not prevent pregnancy, because some semen can leak out earlier.)

"I won't tell anyone."

"I'll respect you even more."

Lines That Threaten You with Rejection

"If you don't have sex, I'll find someone who will."

Lines That Attempt to Gain Sympathy

"Start crying if she says no—it works," says one student.

"Now you have me hot and bothered."

"I'm a virgin and I've got six months to live."

"If a man gets too frustrated, it can fall off."

Lines That Flatter

"You're one of the most beautiful women I've ever seen and I would be honored to spend the night with you."

Lines That Attempt to Put Down the Refuser

"You're such a bitch."

"You obviously have no respect for your body."

"Grow up, Pollyanna."

"Are you frigid?"

"You're really old-fashioned."

"You're not normal."

"Are you gay?"

Lines That Stress the Beautiful Experience Being Missed

"Our relationship will grow stronger."

"Life is so short—let's make the most of it."

"Our relationship really needs to move on."

Lines That Might Settle for Less

"Won't you just lie there?"

"I don't want to do anything. I just want to lie next to you."

Lines to Make You Prove Yourself

"If you loved me, you would."

Lines That Attempt to be Logical, but Aren't

"We're both married, so what's the problem?"

"Don't worry, I'm a doctor."

"If you don't like it, we won't have to do it again."

"You're my girlfriend—it's your obligation."

Lines That Attempt to Answer the Religious Argument

"If God knew how good it was going to be, he'd let you."

Lines That Suggest a Business Arrangement

"I'll let your drug debt slide if you sleep with me."

Lines That Are Totally Transparent

(If you believe either of these, you are extremely vulnerable to deception and might need to seek counseling to avoid being exploited.)

"I'll say I love you after we do it."

"I swear I'll get a divorce."

Many of these lines are hilarious when taken out of a passionate sexual context. It's hard to believe that anyone would fall for them. But in the midst of passion some of them seem, if not perfectly appropriate, at least temporarily believable.

Sol Gordon is a sex educator who combines academic knowledge with a down-to-earth approach in his book, *Seduction Lines Heard 'Round the World and Answers You Can Give*. He's quick on the uptake, and recommends humorous retorts for various situations, mostly for people who are interested in turning off someone else's advances:

> *Female:* Sex isn't such a big deal. What are you waiting for?
>
> *Male:* I'm waiting for someone it's a big deal with.

> *Female:* You should be flattered. I don't give my body to everyone.
>
> *Male:* I wouldn't want to ruin your record.

> *Male:* I feel like an animal when I'm around you.
>
> *Female:* Should I spread some newspaper?[19]

Sol Gordon's retorts are amusing. Not everyone can think that fast or be that witty. But the major problem with put-down retorts is this: If someone to whom you are not attracted tells you a seductive line, that's easy. It's when you *are* attracted (and maybe aroused) that the line may have more effect on you. You may tend to believe the lines because

- you are so aroused you'd like any excuse to proceed.

- you are so crazy about her you'd believe anything she said.

- you have come from a caring family background where people told the truth, and you just naturally believe it when someone says something loving to you.

Remember, recent surveys show that up to one-half of young Americans *admit* they will lie to get sex. (That's who actually *admit* it—we believe the number who really *would* lie is much larger.) No doubt many singles in their thirties and forties would also distort their disease history. Even though men are the traditional seducers, women don't always tell the truth either. Some women have lied to entrap or hurt someone.

You may find you can use what I'm saying to shore up cynical beliefs about getting involved. If you think men or women are untrustworthy and relationships are always risky, you can quote parts of this book and reinforce that belief. But that is not the point. There is a wide range of people with whom you could form deep and loyal relationships. There are truthful people who wouldn't intentionally lie to hurt someone. But I'm trying to get you to

- become a bit skeptical if you're an overly trusting type.
- learn to tell the difference between safe and unsafe sexual situations.

IDEAL SEXUAL ASSERTION

In their manual, *Behavioral Group Intervention to Teach AIDS Reduction Skills*, Jeffrey Kelly and Janet St. Lawrence list some important things you need to include if you're trying to be sexually assertive.[20] These techniques are based on learning theory, and they are scientifically sound ways to change behavior. Kelly and St. Lawrence suggest that you:

1. Acknowledge the other person's position. That is, if you're in a situation where another person is pushing you with words, you can let him know you understand his viewpoint:

"I know you'd like to keep going."

"I know you don't like condoms."

"I hear you, you think people should have sex whenever they want to, no matter how long they've known each other."

2. Clearly refuse the other person's unreasonable demand:

"I won't have intercourse outside of a committed relationship."

"I won't have sex without a condom."

3. Explain the reason you are refusing the unreasonable request:

"Because I think in the nineties it's too risky for disease."

"Because I would not be comfortable with myself if I did."

"Because it's against my religious beliefs."

Kelly and St. Lawrence further suggest that you tell your partner whether there's an alternative or solution acceptable to you. That is, if you won't do A or B to get sexual satisfaction, is there a safer alternative? If so, be specific when talking to your partner.

YOUR POLICY STATEMENT

If you were about to climb a mountain cliff with someone you did not know—where there was some danger, but reaching the top might be exhilarating—would you just tie on the ropes and take off up the cliff with her? No, you'd probably check out what kind of person she is, how she feels about climbing, who's going to go first, how much you might help each other. To begin with, you might tell her what you think about climbing cliffs. And you'd be looking quite carefully at her gear to see whether it was adequate for your protection as well as hers. You would listen carefully to her policy about safety.

Schools, churches, and even countries make policy statements. They spend much time perfecting these statements, and the good policy statements are as precise as possible. Long experience has taught them the importance of taking a clear stand on vital issues.

People who know they're close to becoming sexually involved need to let their partners know their policies about sex. Your date can no longer assume that you hold the policy, "Nice women don't and men probably will." If you are older or divorced, you have no doubt realized that many dates assume you are sexually available. Women now have another kind of equality with men; now neither one has a built-in excuse to refuse sex.

Today, in the nineties, no one can assume anything about your sexual beliefs and standards (your "policy"). You could believe premarital sex is wrong, or you could believe sex is a form of recreation. You could believe in equal sexual rights, or you could believe that one gender exists for the sexual pleasure of the other. People in our society hold a most amazing, and rather scary, variety of sexual attitudes.

Partners will need to bring up the subject of sex *before* sexual involvement might occur—and let the other person know where they stand. All the experts on sexually transmitted disease and acquaintance rape recommend this plan. Our society has too many conflicting messages about sex for people to make any assumptions about another person's sexual intentions. Such suppositions are no more accurate than mind-reading.

Keep another issue in mind as well. Unless you have "total sexual nonresponse" (don't feel at all interested in sex) when you're touching someone to whom you're attracted, that person will know if you're aroused. *Your partner needs to know what that arousal means and how far you will go with it.* The confusion over how far a partner wants to go is becoming a very serious matter in the United States. Numerous surveys, for example, show that men who rape acquaintances often believed she meant "yes" when she said "no." You're living in a society where sexual confusion is the norm.

The kind of words the couple use here could be very important. You may be passionately kissing and petting and say, "I don't want to go further." That may not be literally true, you probably do want to, physically. It may be that you don't *intend* to, that you *plan* not to, that you *believe* it is not best. It may help the partner to know that even if your body seems to want to go further, your mind has decided something else. It sounds like a small thing, but it's critical with some people; the situation is set up for a partner to interpret passion as intention to have intercourse. Being aroused, even in the nineties, does not always signal your intention to go further.

Let's say Lauren and Keith are sitting in her living room. They've been kissing and they're beginning to pet with clothes on. Lauren doesn't intend to have intercourse at this time, even though she would like to. She thinks it would feel great, but she is popular and has dated a lot, and is looking for a long-term relationship. As attracted as she is to Keith, she realizes that she can't go to bed with everyone she dates a few times.

Lauren: (Sits back on the couch for a moment) You feel so good. (She smiles)

Keith: You, too.

Lauren: I need to...talk a minute...I...guess you may be wondering what's going to happen between us. I'm very attracted to you. (She touches his hand, smiles.) I like this, it's great. But I need to let you know how far I intend to go with it. I don't want you to misunderstand what I want to do with you...(She stops to look for his reaction. He's listening. So far, so good.) You know what I mean?

Keith: Yeah.

Lauren: I like you a lot and...I'd like to keep seeing you. I'd like to see what develops between us. But...I've decided I can't...go to bed with someone, I can't have sex with someone I'm just dating. I'd have to be...steady for quite awhile or serious about someone to go that far. (She looks at him, concerned.) I hope you understand what I'm saying.

What Keith says at this point could go any of several ways. A mature person who is capable of seeing another person's viewpoint would listen and understand what she's saying. He might make a few persuasive remarks, but would finally accept her limits. Or he might say he is not interested in waiting and wants a different kind of relationship.

But an immature person—of whom there are many—might really have trouble understanding another person's sexual rights. People who try to manipulate others with "lines," for example, are immature—like a child who is lying to get a treat. People who want what they want when they want it lack what we call "the ability to postpone gratification." Most people like sex—but demanding it from another person or becoming furious when they refuse is immature.

Let's see how Lauren could react to Keith:

Lauren: (Continues to finish her policy statement.) I'd like to keep dating you, I really like you. I love to kiss and...do what we're doing tonight. But I'll have to stop when it comes to keeping our clothes on. That kind of helps me to keep it under control, you know what I mean?

Keith: Yeah, I think so...(frowns).

Lauren: So that's what I'd like to have happen between us, to keep dating and not to go further than we have tonight. (She looks at him, concerned about his reaction, and smiles.) Would that be...would you agree to have a relationship like that for a while?

Here, Lauren has done two things:

1. She's told him her policy. She could be even more explicit, so that there is no room for misunderstanding: exactly what is she willing to do and exactly where does she want to stop?

2. She's asked him for the kind of relationship she wants to have right now, and asked him whether he agrees. Experts in the field of human relations urge partners to specify exactly what they want to do in a relationship and ask the other person to agree to it out loud. They should not assume that their understandings are clear. Asking for what you want and getting the agreement of the other person to do that with you is a kind of unwritten "contract."

Sex educators in the nineties often advise that a couple find safe ways to become sexually satisfied—ways that do not entail any sexual risk. What you are willing to do can become part of your policy statement.

AROUSAL AND GUILT

Some partners feel uncomfortable resisting pressure, as if they were somehow *depriving* their companions. "Naughty me for not giving you what you want." American women pick up the idea that they shouldn't deprive men, and men may feel confused about staying in a relationship without intercourse because *there are no models for adult males to date in this society without sexual inter-course*. Our models tell us that since abstinence is frustrating, "real grown-ups" *of course* have sex when they're dating. But this view-point means one thing to the couple who has been going out steadily for a year, and quite another to the popular person who has three dates every week.

HOW MEN CAN RESPOND TO PRESSURE

Some college counselors report a surprising number of young men who are worried about sexual pressure from women. It is so unac-ceptable to refuse a woman that these men become anxious and concerned about their sexuality. They wonder if there is some-thing wrong with them because they don't want to go as fast as their partners do. Some homosexuals may have similar concerns but are often afraid to ask for professional help.

We need to rethink what it means to be a man. A real man can use his brain and not always his body. A real man can turn down a fight and should be complimented for having the strength to solve a problem nonviolently. A real man can decide whether it's wise to have sex with a particular partner. He can base his sex-ual decisions on the reality of the situation and not on the advice of his locker room pals or his buddies at work. Men are truly among the brainwashed. They are not only brainwashed to assume that they can't turn down sex, but they are brainwashed to believe they have no self-control. *Up to half of American adolescents agree that rape is justified if a female "gets a male too aroused" and stops!* To show fur-ther how confused we are on this subject, surveys that ask, "Have you ever forced intercourse on someone?" find higher rates of agreement than surveys that ask, "Have you ever raped someone?" The implication is that force is to be expected, but really isn't rape unless it's a rare case involving special circumstances.

Many men do not realize what a tremendous put-down it is to portray men as sexually out-of-control. Our culture is so enamored of the image of the muscle-bound hunk that the idea of a male being barely under control seems somehow complimentary. "Real potent guys" can barely hold back. But it is *not* complimentary. Men with a high sex drive may be proud of their sexual capacity, but to stress that it's barely under control implies that men are not trustworthy and can't be held responsible. This concept shores up the belief that men should lay careful battle plans to "score" against the opponent, women. More experienced men are sometimes able to think of assertive responses to risky sexual propositions. What are some of their suggestions for how to resist pressure?

> *She:* I don't want to have sex with you—I want to *make love* to you.
>
> *He:* I know, and I'm attracted to you, you know I am. But I'm just not ready to get that involved right now.

> *She:* Come on, honey. Are you afraid or something?
>
> *He:* It's much more than that. It's an important decision. This is really...great, but I like to control my own decisions.

> *She:* Do you have some kind of sexual problem?
>
> *He:* I hope you don't start questioning my manhood just because I want to make my own choices.

Saving Face in the 'Locker Room'

Males need to learn how to assert themselves when other males pressure them to be more sexual than they want, or to brag about sexual conquests. Teenage males, especially, may brag about their conquests, but some men don't outgrow this tendency. Gayle M. Stringer and Deanna Rants-Rodriguez suggest ways that guys can change how they respond to the "locker room bragging."[21]

> *A says:* Who was that fox?
>
> *B replies:* Janice was the girl I was with.

> *A asks:* Did you score?
>
> *B replies:* Hey, I wasn't playing a game.

A says: Was she any good?

B replies: We always have a great time.

Or: She's a lot of fun to be with.

A says: What's the matter, doesn't sex turn you on?

B replies: Sure, it turns me on, but my private life is my own business and it's not something I want to talk about with everybody.

How can men say no, or say that they want to postpone sex? In class role-plays college men being pressured by a woman often go on trying to resist for a few minutes, like this:

Male: No, you're pressuring me.

Female: Come on, what's bothering you?

Male: Nothing, I just need to wait.

Female: What's your problem, honey?

Male: Well, I...have another girlfriend.

The man says the last line, which could also read, "I'm moving out of town," when he runs out of excuses. One young man turned to me after the woman had pressured him for about one minute and said, "Help!" It is so rare for a man to turn down sex that there just is no vocabulary for it. Or, at least, nothing that could be said in front of other males.

I've noticed that the older the man who role-plays, the better job he generally does in giving her good reasons, such as:

"I'm just not ready yet."

"Don't rush me, I want to take my time."

"No, I want to wait before I get that involved."

One reason men are better at this when they get older could be partly that their self-esteem doesn't depend on what their buddies think. Teenage males tend to be afraid of their peers' disapproval. But a "real man" does not give others that much power over him. A mature man does not conduct his sex life for the approval of his buddies.

The Double Bind

Sometimes confusing messages put men into what we call a "double bind." This is a term for being in a conflict with another person but not being able to talk to her to resolve it.[22]

The double bind can be seen in the proverbial joke about the mother who bought her son two shirts. He wore one shirt. When she saw him in it, she protested, "What's the matter, you didn't like the other shirt?" Since he couldn't wear two shirts, he was in a bind. Because he couldn't talk to his mom to resolve the issue, he was in a *double* bind.

Just being aroused and having to use your brain to be sensible is, in itself, a bind. But if you're aroused and need to talk about something *and* believe you cannot speak about it, this is a *double* bind.

There are other sexual situations that put a person into a double bind. For example, an incestuous parent is supposedly there to protect the very child he is exploiting. This is a double bind for the child, who cannot ask for protection from his own parent. A partner who gives come-on messages to another and then says "No" puts the other into a bind. Which one does she mean?

If a woman seems to be saying "No" and a man feels she really means "Yes," he should get out of this double bind by asking, not by pushing:

> *A:* No, I can't, don't...
>
> *B:* (Pulls back and looks at her) I keep feeling that you want to keep going, but you keep saying "No." I don't want to do anything you really don't want to do.
>
> *A:* Well, I...I don't want you to think less of me.
>
> *B:* I won't think less of you whatever you do, but I need to know what you really mean. It's tough to stop now, but I need to know what you want.

If you have the skills to be sexually assertive and believe you can get your feelings across to the other person, you can avoid many sexual double binds.

HOW WOMEN CAN RESPOND TO PRESSURE

There's no reason why women and men could not say essentially the same things in responding to pressure. Most suggestions of what to say apply to either sex. True, women don't have to defend their femininity as often as men may defend their manhood, and men can't specifically say they're afraid of getting pregnant. But the basic reasons to refuse or postpone sex are the same.

Here are some possible replies to some of the pressure "lines" described earlier in this chapter:

He: Don't worry, I'm sterile.

She: I know you want to make me feel safer, but...well, I'm just not comfortable having sex without a condom. I've known a few people who were more fertile than they thought.

He: You can't get pregnant the first time.

She: Hey, where did you get your sex education? People can get pregnant any time they have intercourse, even if it's just for one second.

He: Don't worry, I'll pull out.

She: I know you want to reassure me, but people can get pregnant that way, even without ejaculating.

Or, if you're on the pill: I'm not comfortable with the idea of having intercourse without a condom on all the time.

He: If you don't have sex, I'll find someone who will.

She: I'm really shocked that you would threaten me like this. I need you to really listen and consider my feelings.

Or: I can't believe you are making a threat like this. I'm furious that you would treat lovemaking like some kind of a job, as if anyone will do.

A: I'm a virgin and I've only got six months to live.

B: I certainly hope you can find someone to give you the experience you think you need. But I have to do what is best for me. Sex is not a charity donation.

A: You're such a bitch.

B: It's hard to believe you want to make love to me and you think calling names will put me in the mood. I need to leave, now.

(Remember, a name-caller is more likely to be an acquaintance rapist.)

A: Are you frigid?

B: I can't believe you mean that. I really get turned off when you put me down.

Or: I resent being called names just because I tell you what I want to do with my body.

Or: I really get mad when you question my sexuality just because I want to make my own choices about going to bed.

A: Our relationship will grow stronger.

B: I know you really would like to get more involved right now. But I need to wait. And lots of people have had their relationship grow stronger without intercourse.

A: I don't want to do anything. I just want to lie next to you.

B: The way we're attracted to each other, I don't think that would be a good idea. As much as I care about you, I'd better not spend the night.

A: If you loved me, you would.

B: You know I care a lot about you. But I feel very pressured when you try to get me to do something I'm not ready for. It's not fair to me. Please consider my feelings.

> *A:* You're not considering *my* feelings—you are selfish.
>
> *B:* Too bad I can't do what we both want, but we both want different things this time.

> *A:* You're my girlfriend—it's your obligation.
>
> *B:* If you think sex is an obligation, we need to think about this relationship right now.
>
> (W*atch out* for any such talk—it is very common in abusers and rapists. At best, it's an irrational comment by an immature person.)

> *A:* I'll say I love you after we do it.
>
> *B:* 'Bye, now. (There is no way to deal with a person who would say such a thing. If you stay in a relationship with such a person, lots of luck. Try the counseling advice in the Appendix.)

YOUR BODY IS NOT DEBATABLE

Some people believe that to resist sexual pressure you have to come up with reasons. So it follows, if your partner gives a good reason, you'd better have a good answer for every reason. Or else. Suppose you are not a very wordy person and you're out with someone who puts a lot of verbal pressure on you. You don't have to engage in a debate! *You don't have to say anything except "I don't want to."* It's your body. It's not as if he's asking you to lend him an object that you own. Your body is not an object.

> *A:* Come on, you know we'll use protection. Come on, it's natural.
>
> *B:* No, I've decided it's not a good idea. No.
>
> *A:* But why? Come on, what's your problem? You know I'm safe.
>
> *B:* I don't want to.
>
> *A:* But...there's no reason. I don't understand you!
>
> *B:* That is a reason. I don't want to. I like you a lot, but I just want to have a good time and stop at this point.

That's what you have to get straight: if you don't want to (or if you don't *intend* to, to be more exact), that *is* your reason.

Or you can even say, "I don't know exactly why, really, but I just feel this way." Imagine if someone wanted you to try to eat a food you did not want.

> *A:* Come on, please try it, you'll like this kind of vegetable.
>
> *B:* No, I don't want any.
>
> *A:* But...why not? What's your problem? It's delicious.
>
> *B:* Well, the color, maybe slightly the odor, the experience might not agree with my digestion.
>
> *A:* That's no reason. The color is great. Please, please have some. You haven't given a good reason.
>
> *B:* Well, let me try to explain....I guess it's because I feel...etc.

You wouldn't do that—you'd just say, "I don't want any." *You do not owe anybody an explanation when you say no to sex, either.* Yes, it may be harder to turn down sex than Brussels sprouts. If you want to offer explanations, if you think it's appropriate to the situation, then do so. But you don't *have* to explain. Take a deep breath and remember your rights.

HOW TO DEAL WITH BEING REJECTED

A big fear of which people may not even be totally aware when they're being assertive is the fear of being rejected. "If I come on strong, she might just tell me to get lost." Or, "If I say what I want, I'll hurt his feelings and he won't like me anymore." Or, "If I tell her I want to wait, she'll accuse me of being weak or something terrible."

The bottom line is, you *must* be able to tolerate the idea of being rejected in order to be assertive. For that reason, Chapter 3 discusses the right mental attitude. A dialogue runs inside your head all the time. Here's how that fear of rejection comes up in your self-talk:

She: Come on, Bill, I want you so much.

He: I'm attracted to you, too. I'd just like to wait awhile. I'm not ready for going that far. (I hope she doesn't put me down for that. Is that a frown on her face?)

She: But...I'm not asking for you to do anything you don't want to, but don't you want me? (Is there something wrong with me? God, I'd like to have sex with him. Maybe I can talk him into it.)

He: Yes, I want you...but not right now. It's too soon. (I wonder if she'll tell everyone?)

She: You know, you're downright insulting. Am I ugly or something?

He: I don't mean to insult you. I'm very attracted to you, and I'd like to get to know you better. (Damn, she's going to push me on this. I feel so uncomfortable. But I'm doing the right thing.)

No one likes rejection. But you can live through it if you don't make it a catastrophe. Remember, you're worth protecting and you're worth taking care of. A respectful person listens to you and cares about your feelings. Anyone who would reject you just because you don't take care of his or her sexual needs is making a totally self-centered statement.

How Would You Reply?

Practice what you would say, in your own words, to reply to the statements below:

"Why not? We both need it." You reply:

"We'll use protection, it's okay." You reply:

"But I thought you loved me!" You reply:

"Are you a child or a woman?" You reply:

"Are you a man or a boy?" You reply:

"Is something wrong with me, aren't you attracted to me?" You reply:

"But I have *needs*!" You reply:

"It's only a natural act, it doesn't mean anything." You reply:

"Grow up, little girl." You reply:

"Let me show you how much I love you." You reply:

"Now you have me all hot and bothered." You reply:

"Don't worry, honey. I'm on the pill." You reply:

"I know you're a normal guy, and you're attracted to me. What's wrong?" You reply:

The very act of coming up with your own answers will help you learn ways to talk back to sexual pressure. It will also help you to become aware when someone tries to manipulate you, so that you develop the protective "part" of yourself that looks out for you. Even if you become sexually involved with an honest and fair person, that person's interest may not be the same as yours. Or that person might be impulsive some time when *you* need to stop and be thoughtful. You must always check with your own feelings and be able to talk about them.

CHAPTER FIVE

Speaking Up to Avoid Disease and Pregnancy

Lust makes you stupid.[23]

—"Sylvia" (Nicole Hollander)

We inherit one connection that is absolutely basic: the link between sex and pleasure, between sex and being alive. To avoid sexually transmitted disease, we have to make a giant mental leap: *we also have to connect sex with pain or death.* There is something inherently unnatural about that connection; it goes against our biological programming. The human race does not seem very proficient at connecting death (or even pregnancy) as an outcome of sexual intercourse.

This chapter will help you learn how you or your partner can avoid acquiring a sexually transmitted disease (STD) or becoming pregnant. It is not only for those who have no STDs at present, since people infected with one disease can acquire other STDs. That's another mental distortion: the idea that lightning can't strike twice in the same place.

HOW WIDESPREAD ARE THE STDS?

The following chart shows the major STDs in the United States and their symptoms.

Six Sexually Transmitted Diseases:

	CHLAMYDIA	GONORRHEA
CAUSE	Chlamydia trachomatis bacterium	Neisseria gonorrheae bacterium
SYMPTOMS IN WOMEN	Usually no symptoms; occasional vaginal discharge	Usually no symptoms; occasional vaginal discharge or painful urination
SYMPTOMS IN MEN	Usually discharge and painful urination	Usually discharge and painful urination
WHEN SYMPTOMS USUALLY APPEAR	1 to 30 days after exposure	1 to 10 days after exposure
SOME POTENTIAL CONSEQUENCES IF UNTREATED	Various inflammations, including pelvic inflammatory disease in women, which can lead to sterility	Various severe complications, including pelvic inflammatory disease in women, which can lead to sterility
SOME POTENTIAL CONSEQUENCES TO INFANTS BORN TO INFECTED MOTHERS	Eye infections and pneumonia	Severe eye infections

Warning Signs*
(*other symptoms may occur—seek medical advice to be certain)

GENITAL WARTS	HERPES	SYPHILIS	AIDS
Human Papilloma virus: HPV	Herpes Simplex Virus Types I and II	Treponema pallidum bacterium	Human immunodeficiency virus: HIV
Single or multiple soft, fleshy growths around anus, vulva, vagina, or urethra. Painless	Single or multiple blisters or sores on genitals. Generally painful but disappear without scarring; may reappear	Four stages: 1) painless chancre—red spot later forming a sore; 2) skin rash or mucous patches; 3) latent stage, no symptoms; 4) complications leading to possible death	After initial infection, may be asymptomatic for years. HIV-related illness progresses to symptomatic phase: fatigue, poor appetite, weight loss, diarrhea, night sweats; the last phase is AIDS, in which other infections cannot be resisted by damaged immune system.
Single or multiple soft, fleshy growths around anus, penis, or urethra. Painless	Same as for women	Same as for women	Same as for women
1 month to 1 year after exposure	1 to 3 weeks after exposure	2 to 4 weeks after exposure	May have no symptoms for years but can still infect others
Some studies show it may cause cervical cancer in women	Cervical cancer believed to be more common in infected women	Death. Disease rarely progresses this far today	HIV infection progresses more rapidly to AIDS (Acquired Immune Deficiency Syndrome) without treatment. Death
Growth could obstruct birth canal	Infection of infant. Caesarean delivery may be advised	Death, bone deformities, nerve disorders	Some infants will be infected and go through same stages as above

The Centers for Disease Control estimate that *every year* in our country there are:

1,500,000 new cases of gonorrhea

500,000 new cases of genital herpes

110,000 new cases of syphilis

4,000,000 new cases of urethritis and chlamydia

1,000,000 new cases of genital warts

1,000,000 new cases of nonspecific, pelvic inflammatory condi tions that result in over 100,000 cases of sterility every year

These are only some of the major diseases. The CDC estimates 4,000,000 new cases of other sexually transmitted disease *every year*, not including HIV, the virus that causes AIDS.

One symptom of a sexually transmitted disease is a burning sensation when urinating, but the absence of such signs does not necessarily indicate health. The experience of Bill and Lisa, two university students who had been dating for several months, shows how disease may be silent in one partner and show up only when the other partner becomes infected. Bill began to have difficulties with painful urination, but despite repeated treatment with antibiotics, the symptoms persisted. His disease, chlamydia, now the most widespread bacterial STD in the United States, can cause sterility and be passed on to newborns.

Unaware that she carried chlamydia, Lisa was not treated until Bill had failed several times to get rid of it. He had received several rounds of antibiotics from a couple of doctors before he recovered. Now Lisa and Bill are both fine, but they could have prevented the disease.

Many STDs go undetected because the victims don't *notice* their symptoms, or there *are* no noticeable symptoms. Note that complications such as pelvic inflammatory disease, sterility, or danger to the infants of pregnant women, in addition to potentially fatal infections, may result from undetected or untreated STDs. Less than half of the women with gonorrhea observe any symptoms. We now believe that herpes may have infected people who are unaware of it. The sores of syphilis may be painless and disappear, while the person is still infected. The partner with whom you're considering having intercourse could even be a carrier of more than one disease and not know it. Researchers estimate that one person could possibly acquire as many as five sexually transmitted diseases in one act of intercourse. Unlikely? Yes. But this claim dramatizes the possibilities and destroys the myth that people with one STD cannot get another one. All of the STDs are treatable, and most are curable. Seek medical advice if you or your partner has any of the symptoms on pp. 78–79.

Attraction

I can make you an absolute, ironclad guarantee: anyone to whom you are sexually attracted seems totally disease-free.

Not only that, but I can assure you that if you become sexually involved and use condoms, after a while—with no test or further reassurances—it will seem perfectly natural and safe to stop using protection because you "know" your partner. However, your lover could be just as infected as when you were careful. Nothing has changed except your belief.

In moments of passion, that person seems, if not decent and honorable, at least irresistibly magnetic and safe. Becoming further involved, letting your body feel everything it wants to, seems wonderful, beautiful, delicious, and the only reality.

In the sixties and seventies, for the first time in human history, "the pill" freed millions of people from worry about pregnancy. For the first time, life seemed to promise that they could at last enjoy sex to the fullest without any undesirable consequences. But even then, sexually transmitted diseases were taking their toll. Long before AIDS, millions suffered from the other STDs. It has just taken more openness as the years pass for us to face the rising STD rate. STD has been a secret between doctor and patient, or a secret shared with no one, or not even recognized as a disease by the person harboring it.

FINDING YOUR RISK TRIGGERS

Maggie loves desserts. The times she most wants dessert are when she finishes dinner or comes home very hungry in the afternoon.

These events trigger her sweet tooth, and her desire usually centers on chocolate, but, in a pinch, she'll settle for anything sweet. If she sets up a fruit dessert at those times, however, and keeps her favorite goodies out of the house, she eats very little dessert but is still satisfied.

I used to help my clients to quit smoking. We spent a lot of time listing their triggers—the situations in which they wanted a cigarette. For some, it was the end of a meal or talking on the phone. Others associated a drink with cigarettes. In order to become nonsmokers, they learned new ways to avoid their old triggers, things that lured them into old habits in an automatic, thoughtless way.

This concept also applies to avoiding STDs. It is very important when breaking a habit to find your triggers. Getting into high-risk situations rather than having low-risk sex is something you *can* control, just as a person wanting to eat healthy food doesn't stare at the junk food machine when he's hungry.

If you take sexual risks, you need to trace back to discover what kinds of situations foster your high-risk behaviors. Does hanging out in bars trigger your making sexual contacts or going home with someone? Do you have fantasies of high-risk behaviors but never fantasize about safer sex? Do you hang out with a gang who brag about their sexual conquests and pressure you to "tell all"?

Among the major triggers for high-risk behavior is taking a mind-altering chemical such as alcohol. If you use chemicals during times when a relationship might become sexual, all the good intentions in the world may not give you good judgment. I know a young woman who has had five STDs. She has several drinks when she's out at night, but she doesn't make the connection that normal inhibition—her normal resistance—is lowered every time she drinks. Many of these chemicals have the same effect; they shut down good judgment. This is one reason why so many crimes involve alcohol. If you think you may be in a situation where you're tempted to have sex, find something nonalcoholic to drink and eliminate any other mind-altering drugs. You want to keep the rational part of your brain in its best working order.

To see whether you have any triggers, fill in the blank with as many actions as you can:

When I _____ I find that I don't protect myself as well as I can from sexually transmitted diseases.

How many triggers fit that sentence for you? You may want to make a list of your triggers so they become a reality to you rather than a trance-like stimulus of which you're barely conscious. A trigger can be somewhere you go, something you do, some drug that you take, or certain people you choose. And your age or sexual preference does not matter—anyone can have triggers.

For example, John, a gay male, says his triggers are drinking alcohol with a sexually attractive acquaintance, and hanging out in bars where people make sexual contacts. Casual sex is taken for granted in many bars. Both of these practices, by the way, often trigger risky sex for heterosexuals as well.

MOTHER NATURE'S PLAN

Mother Nature does not like to be fooled. She determined millions of years ago that, really, she had but two goals for you: one was to keep you alive, safe from serious dangers such as being gored by the buffalo, and the other was to get you (or your girlfriend) pregnant. She devised a terrific pair of the rosiest-colored glasses through which you have to look every time you "see" your partner. She fixed it so you will never take off those glasses as long as you're passionately attracted to that partner.

Unfortunately, disease is a hitch in nature's plan. We have a sex drive, but we don't have a drive to avoid STDs, because the drive to reproduce tends to overpower any other considerations. We have other built-in protective tendencies, such as the tendency to dislike bitter foods (which might contain poison) or to blink our eyes when something comes hurtling toward us. But the strong motive for sexual reproduction leaves us with nothing to protect us from disease except one thing: *our brain's ability to plan ahead and project events that have not happened.*

Studies show that at least one-half of single people take major sexual risks. One of the greatest risks is lack of caution with new partners. And many people take a risk after "getting to know" the person for a while, when they stop using condoms.

Part of nature's plan to get people pregnant causes another mental distortion that blocks good judgment. That is called the *personal fable*. It is the belief that "it can't happen to *me*." *I* can't get pregnant, *I* can't really get a disease, *I* can't die. Even married women who get pregnant for the first time report a certain amazement that it's actually happened to them.

I am taking the chance of scaring you a bit to motivate you to take the problem seriously. But the evidence from smoking and other habit changes is that *just scaring* people is not enough. Too much fear may turn on their "denial mechanism" so that they shut out any information about dangers.

The tendency to deny unpleasant things is universal. Denial is a mental mechanism that we use to defend ourselves from frightening thoughts; we simply block them out—we deny them. Some people use denial very often, whereas others rationalize, blame, or cope in a healthy, direct way with things that scare them. Denial might be needed sometimes to block out things that prevent us from functioning, but, easily overdone, it can cause us trouble if we refuse to see a risky situation. The fact that a healthy, attractive person could unknowingly carry an invisible disease simply boggles the mind.

THREE BASICS ABOUT STDS

If you forgot everything else, three basic principles about STDs are the most vital for you to understand.

1. *Infection almost always gets into your body by direct contact.* Sitting on toilet seats, trying on bathing suits, or being sneezed on are unlikely to expose you to any live STD viruses or bacteria. While pubic lice can be transmitted through towels or sheets, scientists are doubtful that most STD organisms can live long enough in the open air, and there isn't enough

virus in a sneeze (in the case of AIDS) to infect anyone. Sharing drug needles that come right out of one person's bloodstream and into another's, or receiving an infected blood transfusion (now uncommon due to screening) can carry HIV—the virus that causes AIDS—right into your body. Transmission of STDs typically occurs between the genitals and mucous membranes of body openings (mouth, vagina, or anus). Some diseases are passed when one person's body fluids (such as blood or semen infected with HIV, or fluid from an open herpes lesion) contact another person's cut skin or mucous membranes. Although fever blisters on the mouth do not reveal anything about a person's sexual activities, they are a form of herpes and can be transmitted to the genitals.

2. *Your odds of getting any STD are decreased by proper use of a condom.* Using a latex condom correctly would prevent millions of cases of STD. Because they provide a barrier through which viruses and bacteria apparently cannot travel, latex condoms could save your life or your fertility. But condoms are not a guarantee against infection. Condoms can break; fluids sometimes escape the condom. The spermicide non-oxynol 9 may help to kill viruses that spill over. You have to be careful to use condoms correctly, and you still have to give consideration to the person's sexual history, *if* you know it. Keep up-to-date on the latest information about protection by calling resources in the Appendix. Some medical authorities now recommend the use of double latex condoms with a spermicide, in case one condom leaks or breaks. It is also advisable to buy condoms before traveling outside the United States, since foreign products are unreliable.

3. *There are only two ways you can be sure that you will not get a sexually transmitted disease:* totally avoid risky sexual practices; or, in a committed relationship, be *absolutely* certain neither you nor your partner is infected with anything.

THE MAJOR STDS

You've seen in the chart on pp. 78–79 the causes and symptoms of the most common STDs. After reading it most of us probably want to throw up our hands and say, "Hey, it's in the hands of fate, I can't possibly avoid all that, so why bother?"

It's easier, however, if you remember that *you can largely control your exposure to STDs by learning a few basic things to say and do.*

The fact is, you cannot afford to allow your body to be the conduit for viruses or bacteria from everyone who's slept with everyone who's slept with everyone you've slept with. The following diagram shows you how misleading it can be to have an unprotected sexual relationship with someone whom you know has had no unhealthy contacts.

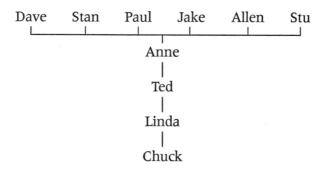

Chuck is having sex with Linda, who has had only one relationship before Chuck. Chuck has had only one relationship, with a sexually inexperienced girl in high school. Linda dated Ted and broke up with him. Without the knowledge of Linda, who was completely faithful to Ted, he had dated Anne, who had numerous lovers and had even experimented with intravenous drugs.

So you have to get this straight in your mind—STDs can happen to you. Anyone exposed by sexual contact to sufficient bacteria and viruses can acquire a sexually transmitted disease. Chapter 3 has shown you some beliefs and rights that you truly need to *integrate and believe in* to be best able to defend yourself.

Long before the moment when two people exchange a disease, there are critical times when they could make different choices. At crucial moments, something could be said or done to protect the individual from an annoying, embarrassing, frightening, or even fatal decision.

Of the factors that can influence the partner to be safe, what is *said* is crucial. Words can powerfully influence what people do, and your words come from the rational part of your brain that is not responsible for leading you into passion. Humans have a unique ability to communicate the most subtle meanings about our desires and needs so we can ask what we want to know about a partner or tell him about ourselves. *On these words may hinge our sexual health, whether we become parents, and maybe even our lives.*

THE FIRST CONVERSATION

Before you ever get into a risky passionate embrace with someone—and want to go further—you can find out a lot about what kind of disease risk she is. In their first conversations, a person of any age can "interview" a potential partner. Listen carefully to how she talks about several topics important to you; be alert to signals of safety and danger in what she says. You may be very powerfully attracted to her, but at the same time another part of your mind can assess how safe she might be in a sexual situation. The person who *denies* danger is the most likely to ignore critical clues from a potential partner.

People wonder, of course, how to bring up the sensitive subject of sex in the first place. How do you start a conversation about sex in general, so that later you could feel more comfortable discussing sex between you two?

One of the best ways to start is to talk about the media: a movie, the newspaper, or TV. That's also a good way to let the other person know what *you* believe about sex. Discuss what's going on in your country, state, city, or school. Listen carefully to the other person's opinions.

For example, let's take Pat and Marc. They have just met and are powerfully attracted to each other. But Pat doesn't want to make a sexual mistake; she wants to find out what kind of sexual values Marc has. She decides to steer the conversation gradually around to sexual matters—but to sexual things that are far removed from herself and Marc—to get to know Marc better.

Pat: Did you see that ball player on the news last night?

Marc: Yeah, I heard he was on drugs big time.

Pat: Well, I saw an article where he said he'd never shoot up because two of his friends had AIDS.

Marc: Huh. Well, ball players, aren't they pretty clean?

Pat: They say it's easy to get AIDS from drug needles that people pass around. (Here, Pat pauses to see what Marc will add.)

Marc: I don't know, maybe that AIDS stuff is just a big scare. I saw on TV the other night that it's all blown way out of proportion.

Pat: (Pat decides to come right out and establish the beginning of a "safer sex" conversation.) Do you really think so? Well, even the government thinks it's serious. I think people should make sure they're safe.

Marc: Hey, it's not much of a problem for most people. Homosexuals already have cut it down and heterosexuals aren't very susceptible.

Pat: I'm surprised you think that; that's not what I heard.

Now Pat has asserted herself to find out that Marc is not well informed. Homosexuals are just as susceptible to HIV infection in risky behavior as they have always been, even though some communities have cut down their AIDS rate by changing sexual practices. And heterosexuals, if they use unsafe sexual practices, have the same rate of infection as any group—we are all susceptible to AIDS.

KEY PHRASES TO REMEMBER

If you are just beginning to talk to an attractive person, it can help to sprinkle into your conversation a few phrases that indicate how you feel or asking your date's opinions about sexual risk. You can revise these in your own words.

"I need you to listen to how I feel about..."

"It would be easy to keep going, but I have to talk..."

"I'm attracted to you, but I'm trying to be..."

"I've been thinking about what I would do if we..."

"How do you feel—are we going too fast?"

"I need to get to know someone..."

All Pat has done in the conversation above is listen to Marc's views and bring up issues on which Marc could comment. Here are some other ways to bring up sex in a conversation with a new partner:

"Did you see (name a soap) last night? What did you think of___?" (I can guarantee there will be some sexual relationship on which you could comment.)

"Did you see that magazine article?"

"Did you see on the news about that woman who...?"

As you listen to a potential partner talk, ask yourself questions:

1. Is this person concerned about disease? Or does she have a nonchalant, carefree attitude based on fun above all? Someone like that can be very attractive but also very dangerous to your health.

2. Is this person honest in his *nonsexual* dealings? Does he try not to hurt other people necessarily, or is he inconsiderate of other people? When talking about politics, job, friends, or family, do you hear this person show *caring* about other people? Or does he take any opportunity for personal gain when no one is looking? These general traits usually carry over to other areas of life.

3. Is this person considerate of *you?* The way you're treated in nonsexual ways probably reflects your partner's basic consideration. If you're always expected to go to the movies that he chooses, for example; or see people that only he likes and

never the ones you like; if you're expected to cater to him with no thought for your needs, he probably will also be sexually disrespectful of you.

Does that sound like you'll have to find a perfect person? What you're looking for is not some kind of ideal person who doesn't make mistakes—you're looking for someone with whom you could trust your sexual health. It's acceptable for your date to have faults like being messy, late, or too quiet. But certain faults are too important to overlook. The simple truth is, many potential lovers have no concern for your welfare, although some of them might seem great fun to go to bed with. You can decide to go ahead and have that fun, or you can decide to use your brain to protect yourself. Yes, you may have to rule out more people from intimacy if you are this particular. But you only have two choices—rule out anyone who seems inconsiderate and who won't protect you, or take a chance, which might be a big chance, of getting an STD, becoming pregnant, or impregnating someone.

EXPLAINING AHEAD OF TIME

It makes protection much easier if you explain ahead of time, before anything passionate happens, how you feel about sexual safety in general. This explanation is similar to the "Policy Statement" in Chapter 4. But here you're telling not just how far you will go, but what you need for sexual safety. Not that you should stop in the middle of the movie and whisper in her ear, "I'm for safer sex." Just find a good time to steer the conversation around to the topic of sex, see what happens, and find your opportunity to say what you think.

For example, let's say Joe and Maria are college students out on their fifth date. They are very much attracted to each other, but they have done nothing more than kiss on their last date. Tonight they're sitting on the couch in her dormitory lounge. Joe picks up the student newspaper, glances at it, and puts it down.

> *Joe:* Wow, there's so much about gonorrhea on the campus now.

Maria: Yes, it's really in the news.

Joe: They say people can have it and not know it.

Maria: I know. My friend's brother has had it twice.

Joe: People really need to be careful. But I think every-one hates to talk about those things. (He makes a face.)

Maria: Yeah. I guess it's hard to—to talk about. (She's obviously going to let him take the lead.)

Joe: I think people should bring the subject up ahead of time and see if they agree.

Maria: Okay. Well, I see what you're saying....

Joe: I've thought some about what kind of relationship I'd like to have, and how to be careful. Want to know what I think?

Maria: Yes.

Joe: I think we should talk about exactly how to protect ourselves if we make love.

Joe is letting Maria know where he stands, and he's also listening carefully to her attitudes. Would she support him in this? Or would she subtly, or directly, try to undermine him?

Don't forget the "Policy Statement" in Chapter 4. You can avoid many misunderstandings if you talk about how far you want to go as soon as your relationship begins to get more passionate and might proceed to risky sex.

MENTIONING PROTECTION WITHOUT ACCUSING

If you've discussed your general views about sex in preliminary conversations, you've laid the groundwork for later intimate talks. Your partner knows how you feel about sexual risks. Now you want to narrow down the focus, because presumably you wouldn't stay in this relationship unless you hoped it might develop further. Your talks become progressively detailed and personal, like the funnel in the diagram below, until you can talk about sex between you two.

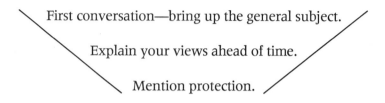

First conversation—bring up the general subject.

Explain your views ahead of time.

Mention protection.

How to be Delicate and Nonoffensive

If you let your partner know you are afraid of disease, any mature person would understand that you're just trying to be sensible and protect both of you. But how can you mention protection with the least possible offense, considering your partner's feelings and preserving the relationship that matters to you?

Starters

It's good to have a few little "starters" to help yourself approach the things you need to say. It's okay to mention your feelings:

> "I need to get more comfortable talking about..."
>
> "I'm not sure I can explain this perfectly, but..."
>
> "It would be easy to go on without saying this..."
>
> "I want to be fair to both of us."
>
> "You know, I see the news and I keep thinking..."

If you are bringing up protection early in a relationship, *you* are right. You are cautious and mature about it; you are doing the honorable thing.

Men in our society are supposed to have courage. The media show examples of supposedly "desirable" courage—killing, hitting, driving fast, courting physical danger. How about the courage to speak up? That takes a lot of bravery and we need to recognize it and admire it. People who speak to their friends about their concerns and say the tough things—I admire those people. Their courage opens an opportunity for others to speak their minds as well:

> "I'm really scared about how you might react, but..."

> "As embarrassing as it is sometimes, I think someone has to have the nerve to speak up."

> "We need to have the guts to talk to each other ahead of time."

IMPERFECT TALK IS OKAY

I'm giving you a lot of material here so that you can absorb various helpful phrases along the way. If you don't put them in this order, if you repeat yourself, and stumble a bit, don't worry about it. You're not a robot or an actor. You might even condense all the important things down to two sentences:

> "I'm not comfortable doing that."

> "If we continue to date, we'll have to stop at this point."

But the more you read and hear about sexual assertiveness, the more it becomes a part of you. In fact, you need to hear yourself say things out loud. If you're reading this on your own, try some practice. Stand in front of the bathroom mirror and *say the things you want to say out loud.* If you need to, take this book with you and go over some of the things you want to be able to say. You could even use a tape recorder in order to hear yourself and begin to integrate that it's really a part of *you* when you talk like this.

You may feel foolish talking to the mirror. (Is she kidding?) No, I'm not kidding. Are we discussing something important, or not? Studies show that people of all ages and backgrounds can remember better if they practice aloud whether they're giving a speech or asking for a raise. They also feel more comfortable later, when they really have to speak their part; it's familiar and they've stored it in memory.

Of course, if you explore the idea in your own words, so much the better. You will feel much more comfortable being sexually assertive in your own natural speech patterns. The acid test of sexual assertiveness is whether you mean what you say, and you say it in a genuine and unaffected way.

LYING IS COMMON

I knew a woman in her late fifties who was lonely, having lost a child and a husband. She met an attractive man; they dated and went to bed without a condom. Afterwards, she spoke to him:

> "You don't have any diseases, do you?"
>
> "I have herpes," he replied.
>
> "Why didn't you tell me?" she exclaimed.
>
> "I always tell people if they ask," he said.

Please don't believe everything a new, attractive person tells you. It is very difficult for many people to admit that they've taken some sexual risks in their past. Even people who are generally honest and caring, when pressed for the precise risk they might have taken, tend to present themselves in the best light. People who want sex with you will be highly motivated to persuade you. Therefore you must proceed as if any new sex partner *could* be infected.

GETTING SPECIFIC

How can *you two* start talking about protection? Let's say Alex and Kelly have been going out together. Kelly has already laid the groundwork by preparing Alex for the conversation about condoms. What happens from here?

If you find a time when you aren't sexually aroused you're more likely to be able to set things up ahead and give your partner time to digest what you've said. Kelly chooses a time when they are not involved in a passionate embrace—perhaps earlier in the evening, alone in the kitchen over a snack.

Kelly: (Takes Alex's hand, rubs a thumb across it) I haven't forgotten what you said last night about...wanting to make love.

Alex: (Grins) I haven't, either.

Kelly: You make me feel really great. I guess you can tell, by the way I talked the other day...that I think people should talk about protection before they get involved.

Alex: Uh, yeah, I remember.

Kelly: Well, I think all that stuff you read about—about using condoms—is right. I think people should use protection. This is kind of hard to say....

Alex: I hope you don't think that I have any—

Kelly: No. That's what makes it so hard to talk about these things, because it sounds like you're trying to accuse someone else of having a disease. Still, anybody could be carrying something and not know it. We could have been lied to, or we could have been with someone who was a carrier and didn't know it.

Kelly tries to reassure Alex. The most mature people respect their partner's reasoning on this subject, but it's usual to push or persuade in the heat of passion and with the prospect of "scoring." If everyone you date is pushy and pretends to be insulted when you're asking for protection, however, if they all treat your sexual opinions with disrespect, that doesn't mean you have to put up with it. It just means you've run into lots of people who are immature. You might want to look at why you're picking such people and where you're picking them.

For example, Jan has met five men in bars and discos, which are the only places she thinks she can "meet guys." Two of them stand her up occasionally and make fun of her for wanting to postpone sexual involvement. The third got so pushy she thought she might be raped, and she did not see him again. The fourth and fifth men wanted sex without emotional commitment. When Jan didn't, they dropped her.

Jan's unhealthy reasoning goes something like this:

"There must be something wrong with me. Or else there's something wrong with men—they can't be trusted." So she continues looking for the right men in bars. Because of her self-concept ("I'm not a goody-goody") she thinks there's nowhere else to meet anyone.

A healthier approach would be, "I've been trying to meet people in only one place. While some nice people may go to bars and discos, they are places where alcohol and loud music make conversation almost impossible. Also, only a small proportion of the guys I might meet go to those places. Could I join a health club or political organization or other group where I would meet a different type of person?"

HOW TO ASK FOR A CONDOM

We left Kelly and Alex beginning to talk about protection. Now they're at the point where it's time to discuss condoms. Remember, a condom is not foolproof. Going to bed with multiple partners *using* condoms subjects you to higher risk of disease than unprotected sex with one healthy partner. The reason for this fact is that condoms sometimes leak or break, and they may fall off if they are not carefully held in place during withdrawal.

Even so, Kelly has decided to have sex with Alex and she wants to minimize the possibility of their transmitting diseases. Their conversation might go like this:

> *Alex:* Okay, what do you want to do?
>
> *Kelly:* Well, I want to use condoms, for one thing. That's about the least couples can do, don't you think?

At this point, Alex may go along with Kelly's plan:

> *Alex:* I agree. Do you want me to buy them?
>
> *Kelly:* Okay, or I can. There's one more thing.
>
> *Alex:* (Laughs) Okay, what?
>
> *Kelly:* They have to be latex and have that spermicide on them.
>
> *Alex:* (Chuckles) Gosh, you've really got it down pat, Kelly.
>
> *Kelly:* (Grinning) I've been readin' up.

But what if Alex is putting pressure on Kelly not to use condoms? What if the conversation went this way:

Alex: A condom! That's like taking a shower in a raincoat.

Kelly: I'm sorry to hear you feel that way. (An I-statement.)

Alex: God, you can't be serious! I can't feel anything that way.

Kelly: I've heard that lots of guys who use condoms feel enough to satisfy them.

Alex: (Now he's in a power struggle and bluffing to see who can win.) Nah, it's not for me.

Kelly: Are you saying, then, that you wouldn't use condoms, no matter what? (Kelly cares about Alex and wants to get it clear before making a decision.)

Alex: Yeah.

Kelly: You're saying you'd rather not go to bed with me at all than to use a condom? (Kelly sounds as if it is unbelievable that Alex would say such a thing.)

Alex: (Frustrated by the truth and maturity of Kelly's statement) You—you don't know what you're talking about! I haven't *got* anything! (Remember, this anti-condom attitude makes Alex *more* likely to have been exposed to an STD in the past.)

Kelly: You know, Alex, I'm not willing to go to bed with someone who puts my life on the line. If you're not willing to do this simple thing to help us both...I guess we're not going to go any further in this relationship.

Alex: You're so selfish!

Kelly: That's merely your opinion. To me, it's caring about myself. I get really mad when you call me names for standing up for myself.

Here Kelly and Alex have arrived at a basic decision. Remember that self-esteem strengthens people to take care of themselves. Kelly may feel very disappointed right now. She was hopeful and excited about her relationship with Alex. But right now freedom from an STD depends entirely on what's going on inside Kelly's head! If she feels able to tolerate being alone for a while, it will be easier to reject Alex. If she can really feel angry about his insults, rather than passively tolerate them, it will be easier to reject Alex. *Because what just happened is that Alex insulted Kelly for trying to protect her body and maybe even her life.*

Psychologists teach people not to label others unfairly. Communication experts emphasize tolerance for the values of other people. But sometimes a label is necessary. A conversation about sex is no occasion to tolerate just any old opinion. Some of us have met so many immature and selfish people that we really don't register a simple fact: there's no future in a relationship with a person who won't even use a condom to protect you both. There may be some temporary fun in it; but recognize the amount of risk and weigh it against the fun.

A Quickie Condom Conversation

If you're a person of few words, of course, there's no need for a long discourse on condoms. Probably quite a few first sexual encounters go like this:

> *A:* Got a condom?
>
> *B:* No.
>
> *A:* Oh, honey, we've got to use a condom.
>
> *B:* Maybe next time?
>
> *A:* No, I really want to use one.
>
> *B:* Nothing can happen right now.
>
> *A:* No. Want to go to the drugstore with me?

Better yet, "A" already has one which she chose because it's the safest and most effective kind of condom.

ASKING FOR BIRTH CONTROL

Asking a partner to use birth control involves the same techniques of assertion as resisting pressure and asking for protection from disease. If you are a woman who is neither on the pill nor using a birth control device, you can check the safety of properly used devices at a local Planned Parenthood or other clinic (see Appendix). But if a man is using condoms to protect you from pregnancy it's best for you to have a say in what kind of condom is used and how it's used. You should tell him pertinent facts about the pill that you are taking. Each of you has an absolute right to know that you are protected, and how. For example:

> *Jane:* I'm glad you bought the condoms. What kind are they?
>
> *Rob:* They're expensive—they're supposed to be good.
>
> *Jane:* Could I see?
>
> *Rob:* (Looks slightly embarrassed) Sure.
>
> *Jane:* (Reading label) Oh, I see they are made of animal skin. I heard that kind aren't as safe because viruses and bacteria might pass through those microscopic holes.
>
> *Rob:* (Looks crestfallen) I tried to get good ones.
>
> *Jane:* I know. When we go out later we could stop by the drug store and exchange them. (She kisses him on the cheek.) Thanks for caring.

I know, this sounds nervy. But she has three choices: use a kind of condom that has been proven less effective, use the safest kind of condom, or avoid sex for now.

If you are a man who is not in a monogamous, trusting relationship, do not trust just any woman to use the pill carefully. Do you want your future as a father to depend totally upon someone's memory to take a few *pills*? Using condoms properly would reduce your concern about her mistakes. *And* using a condom can assure you of greater protection from disease.

Some Helpful Phrases about Contraception

"I really need to use condoms even if you're on the pill."

"I think it's important to double up on birth control."

"I feel very uncomfortable when you keep pressuring me to stop using condoms."

"I'm sorry if it's not what you want, but I need to do this."

TIME OUT! WHAT TO SAY IN THE MIDDLE OF THINGS

Jeffrey Kelly and Janet St. Lawrence are two researchers who have taught a lot of people how to have safer sex.[24] The groups they trained to be assertive have drastically reduced rates of HIV infection. One of their best ideas is to role-play how to stop in the middle of sexual activity if something unsafe is about to happen. They say their research groups found this the most difficult, but also the most helpful role-play, even though it was X-rated. These are some of the kinds of unsafe practices which might start to happen:

Anal sex—it is so highly correlated with HIV infection (the virus that causes AIDS) and hepatitis B that experts simply advise, don't do it. A person having anal sex once in a year greatly increases his chances of HIV infection. Other STDs could also be transmitted anally. This advice applies to heterosexuals as well as homosexuals.

Penetration without protection—condoms must be used before penetration begins and continued throughout intercourse.

Withdrawal without holding the condom in place—condoms may fall off after ejaculation, spilling semen and, with it, viruses or bacteria. Pregnancy can also result from this mistake.

See Appendix for places where you can call to ask about high- and low-risk behaviors. Listed on p. 233 you'll also find a pamphlet that explains little-known hygiene methods to reduce the chances of an infection. And keep informed about new findings concerning all STDs. National hotlines and other places where you can get information about STDs are listed in the Appendix.

There's no way around it, if you are in a sexual situation with someone who tries risky sexual practices, you have to stop it. If you can do it with your body language, fine; if not, you can say, "No!" and move away or otherwise make sure it can't happen. You don't have time to stop and have a conversation.

I also mention how to "stop in the middle of things" for those who are having sex unexpectedly with someone new. Responsible professionals in the field of sexuality advise against multiple sex partners, and sex with someone you do not know is obviously highly risky. Every new partner may increase your risk. But realistically, many people engage in casual sex. Take this moment to imagine that someone is attempting risky sex with you, and picture or hear what you would say and do to protect yourself. Fantasizing is a good method of practicing.

Of course, you can easily figure out a simple phrase to stop things when they're getting risky. But it's good to see some *time-out* statements in writing and to hear them, because your society has never shown them to you:

> "Stop. I need to stop."
>
> "Wait. We haven't taken care of_____."
>
> "Whoops! We almost forgot the condom."
>
> "No. Remember our talk?"
>
> "No, I have to use condoms."
>
> "No. I feel very strongly about this."
>
> "I won't do that."
>
> "I don't want to."
>
> "Time out!"

What if all over America, people who need to stop at any point in sexual arousal would hold up their hands in the T sign of sports and say, "Time out!"? (Well, maybe not in the dark.) I can imagine that this might become a good-natured way of stopping in the name of safe sex, as common a phrase as, "Get off my back!" or "Give me a break!" It would be okay, and expected, and so socially acceptable that everyone would know what it means.

HOW TO ASK FOR AN STD TEST

You may find that this beautiful person before you looks clean as a whistle. But your higher brain knows he could have an STD. There is no test for any STD that couldn't be reversed by the time the test results are in. That is, if Jenny gets tested on Friday, you and she can read the report that she is disease-free on Tuesday; what did she do over the weekend? Trust is still the most vital element in relationships. Mike and Terry are another couple who have been dating awhile and have already talked generally about what they want to do to protect themselves.

> *Mike:* (Sitting on the couch, he has been kissing Terry for half an hour.) I want to make love to you, Terry.
>
> *Terry:* (Smiles dreamily) Me, too.
>
> *Mike:* (Sits back, looks away) God you are so—you just hit me like a ton of bricks. (Runs his finger down Terry's face) I need to talk, though.
>
> *Terry:* Okay. (Smiles)
>
> *Mike:* All the things you read about—I've promised myself that I'll take the time to talk to a new person that I'm starting to care about. I've been reading that...maybe the only way for people to know they're safe...to know that someone hasn't, you know, given them something...is to take a test. (Grins awkwardly) This is hard to talk about.
>
> *Terry:* I hope you don't think that I—
>
> *Mike:* No, no, it isn't you, or me. It's just...the nineties, I guess...a really nice person could have something and not know it.

Or, maybe Terry objects:

> *Terry:* Hey, are you saying I have AIDS?
>
> *Mike:* (Touches Terry's arm) No, I'd never say that to someone I like as much as you. It's just...nobody knows what the people they were involved with before have done. It's getting so...anybody could have anything, I guess. I hate to say it, but how

would I even be sure about myself? Will you go with me to get tested?

There are various tests for a number of STDs. As of this writing there are tests for HIV antibodies in the blood. Keep informed about the latest kinds of tests for STDs and what they mean. Do not assume that some kind of "clean card" carried by anyone has any meaning whatsoever. The only way for a couple to be tested for an STD is to discuss it together with the medical professional, have the test, see each other's test results in the presence of the medical person—*and* totally trust that the partner has not become infected before or since the test was taken. Sometimes HIV, the virus that causes AIDS, can be present in a person's bloodstream, yet not show up on antibody tests for months—or perhaps even years—after infection. However, the Centers for Disease Control state that almost all people will get very reliable test results in three months from the time of infection.

Most physicians do not offer pre- and post-test counseling when they check for HIV, but most government-sponsored testing sites do provide counseling. It is very important to get counseling with HIV test results.

Anyone being tested for HIV infection should be cautious about revealing information concerning the test, regardless of whether the results are positive or negative. Although HIV has never been transmitted by casual contact, there have been cases of discrimination—even when the individual's test was negative. Individuals should inquire ahead of time about confidentiality, without giving their names, before they even consider disclosing any information about their HIV status.

EXERCISES

Respond aloud with an assertive statement to each of the following comments:

"But I don't have any diseases." You reply:

"I don't like to use condoms." You reply:

"It doesn't matter whether they are latex or not." You reply:

"I'll take care of everything—don't worry." You reply:

"You must not trust me or you'd have sex without a condom." You reply:

"Why do you want to talk about all this beforehand? It ruins the spontaneity." You reply:

Some retorts:

"I don't think you have any diseases. I'd say this to anyone. I don't discriminate."

"I don't like **not** using condoms."

"Yes, it does matter. Latex condoms are safer."

"No, I want to be in on everything that affects me."

"I could let myself go a lot more if I felt protected."

"Being spontaneous is easier when I feel safe."

"I'm really disappointed that you won't use protection."

"A condom is a way you show you care about me."

"I have to care about myself, too, you know?"

"I know you'll understand if you really care about me."

IF YOU HAVE EXPOSED SOMEONE TO AN STD

Some STDs are "reportable" and some are not. For example, in most states physicians and private clinics are required to report gonorrhea, syphilis, and HIV infection. The testing site will almost always ask you to contact anyone you may have exposed, and the doctor is supposed to do so as well. *It is extremely important that you contact your partner(s) regardless of whether you are asked to do so.* Because so many people can have an STD and show no symptoms, your telling the truth may be the only way your partner can avoid serious problems. Think how you would appreciate knowing it, if you had been exposed to an STD, so you could obtain medical treatment.

There's no way around just coming out with the truth:

> "I need to tell you something. I went to the doctor yes-
> terday and she said I have chlamydia. She said that I
> need to be sure to tell you so you can see a doctor soon."

You can go on with the facts or pass on a brochure if you have one. Most people, while unhappy with the news, will be glad you've been fair enough to tell them. If anyone gives you a hard time after you tell, you can always say,

> "Would you rather I hadn't told you? This was real hard
> to say, and it didn't do me any good, but I figured it could
> really help you avoid a lot of heartache. I care about you
> and your health."

If you're wondering how to talk about an STD under other circumstances, such as telling a potential partner that you have herpes, you could call one of the resources in the Appendix.

LEGAL ISSUES

If you have an STD and decide to have any risky sexual contact with another person, you should be aware of the legal implications. Attorney Margaret Davis has written a book, *Lovers, Doctors, and the Law*, which details the legal concerns involved in modern sexual relationships.[25]

At this point you may be saying, "Hey, now I know I'm giving up and not worrying about any of it—there's just too much!" Fine, but that doesn't change the reality. A well-informed person who is sexually active in these times has a fairly high chance of having an STD become an issue for him, whether in exposing someone else or being exposed. Even in college classes, it's common for as many as 20 percent to have had an STD scare of some kind.

Lovers, Doctors, and the Law explains the legal responsibilities of partners with and without STDs. There have been a number of court cases in which people who were exposed to an STD without their knowledge have taken ex-lovers and even spouses to court and won.

Davis recommends that you share your medical history with your lover, including the date and findings of your last medical checkup. In addition, she suggests you share information about any previous lovers who had any symptoms of STDs, and any treatment you have had. This precaution in itself might cause you to limit the number of sex partners you have, because how many people do you want to know such personal information about yourself?

In addition, Davis further encourages readers to discuss their recent sex lives and whether either has had any partners from a high-risk group. Again, the answers may be untrue. But a person who lies about his or her disease risk is taking a legal risk, because that person may be found guilty of a civil or a criminal charge.

Davis recommends that lovers make a physical examination for any STD symptoms a part of their foreplay. (This suggestion has been offered by a number of sex educators.) Should you learn anything about the STD history of another person, you are obliged to keep that information confidential. There is a great deal of prejudice, and in some cases risk of discrimination, involved with certain STDs.

DEFEND YOURSELF AND YOUR PARTNER

It is possible for you to be passionately attracted to someone with one "part" of yourself and still be a bit suspicious with another part. Look at it like this: Would you buy a car and not ask anything about its functioning? Would you lend money to someone without inquiring about her dependability? Your body is a lot more important than your car or your money—it is irreplaceable. Respect it enough to protect it.

If you become familiar with assertive actions like those described in this chapter, you're well on your way to being able to defend yourself sexually. Have courage. You're worth it. Nobody has a right to risk your health, and you are the only person who can protect it.

III

HOW TO COPE WITH WITH INTRUSION AND FORCE

CHAPTER SIX

Resisting Sexual Harassment

Power tends to corrupt,
and absolute power corrupts absolutely.

—Lord Acton

"I know how you could make an A in my course."

As implausible as it sounds, sexual propositions from faculty occur with astonishing frequency on college campuses, and even in high schools. And a major study of harassment at work finds that at least one woman in five has quit a job, been transferred, been fired, or withdrawn an application for a job because of sexual harassment.[26]

It is cynical to believe that every powerful person is corrupt. But the political axiom of Lord Acton which begins this chapter strikes at the central motive in all sexual harassment: exploitation of a powerless victim.

WHAT IS SEXUAL HARASSMENT?

According to the dictionary, "harass" means "to vex, trouble, or annoy continually." Always unwelcome, sexual harassment ranges from unwanted sexual innuendos made at inappropriate

109

times—perhaps even in the guise of humor—to coerced sexual relations:

- verbal harassment or abuse
- subtle pressure for sexual activity
- sexist remarks about a person's clothing, body, or sexual activities
- leering or ogling of a person's body
- unnecessary touching, patting, or pinching
- constant brushing against a person's body
- demanding sexual favors accompanied by implied or overt threats concerning one's job or student status
- physical assault

Recent court cases have found employers—including colleges and universities—liable for incidents and conditions in the workplace or on campus that add up to a chilly climate for women. When working conditions make an employee uncomfortable because of the pressure to put up with sexual remarks, gestures, or other uncomfortable sexual events, this too is sexual harassment. For example, if Marie has to sit beside a "nude" calendar all day and listen to people comment on the breasts of the woman on the calendar, her employer can be held liable for not having informed his employees about sexual harassment.

Sexual harassment is unique among the various ways that people can exploit each other. Unlike many other forms of sexual exploitation, *the victim has something to lose on a daily basis*, and the harasser usually knows it. In no other situation except that of marital rape would an adult be expected to tolerate the constant presence of a sexual abuser. As women attain positions of power, they sometimes sexually harass men. But most of the harassment of women and men is done by men—that is, when the victim is a man, he is likely to be the object of homosexual harassment. The advice in this chapter is for anyone facing sexual harassment.

All of the following are examples of sexual harassment:

> Larry, a salesman, needed to sell his product to a woman buyer who made it clear she wanted to go to bed with

him. She said she would not buy his goods if he did not respond. He said: "I did it so she'd buy from me, but she was ugly and repulsive."

Marcia's graduate school professor asked her to stay late to work on some papers. He suggested sex. After she refused, he lowered her grades. The dean who supervised him felt Marcia was exaggerating. She became so upset she transferred to another school and lost a semester's credit.

Tanya, a young single mother of three, worked in a bank. Her employer asked her to stay after work for some extra projects. At first he merely told her how nice she looked. She tried to ignore him. The next time she had to stay late, he put his arm around her waist and tried to kiss her. She pushed him away with a joke. But the next week he called her at home and said she'd better improve her attitude. When she still didn't go along, he asked to have her transferred.

Dan had worked for three years at a good job, and he was up for promotion. But it was obvious that the boss had sexual requirements for moving up in this company, and Lucy, a coworker, qualified. Many workers knew that she and the boss were having an affair, and, although less qualified than Dan, Lucy got the promotion. Dan felt frustrated and angry that he couldn't advance no matter how well he performed at work.

Leslie, a teenager, worked part-time in a small print shop. One day the boss and another employee wrestled her to the floor in the back room and tickled her. They were laughing, although she was screaming for them to stop. Later the other employee apologized, but the boss said she was making a big deal—it was all in fun.

WHAT IS *NOT* HARASSMENT?

Some men are nervous because their behavior with women at work may be misinterpreted. It is unlikely that a person would falsely accuse another of sexual harassment—the accuser usually has little to gain and a lot to lose. But it is a serious matter to accuse someone of an illegal activity which can harm his career. There is much confusion over what constitutes harassment. We need to define our terms carefully.

Having been raised in an affectionate family, I can understand how someone could make a physical gesture with no intention of offending. I often touch friends on the arm, hug them when trying to reassure them about something, or welcome them with an embrace when they return from vacation. If I were a man in a position of power, I would have to be careful about these gestures at work or I might be accused of harassment. On the other hand, being a woman, I know it would be unusual for someone to accuse me of victimization. Men who victimize put other men at risk.

Some people say that this risk of being falsely accused is the price men have to pay for what they have done throughout the centuries. But I do not like the idea of inherited guilt. If an individual man respects women, his attitude is a powerful asset to society, to women, and to men. While we don't inherit guilt, we do inherit responsibility; it is the duty of everyone to speak up against the underlying attitudes that support the sexual sickness of our society. Chapter 10 will address those solutions. Here the discussion focuses on methods to prevent harassment or stop it in its initial stages.

THE PRICE SOCIETY PAYS

Sexual harassment causes the loss of millions of dollars to American industry. After surveying 20,000 federal employees, the Merit Systems Protection Board estimated the cost of harassment to be $189 million, resulting from job turnover, stress, absenteeism, and reduced productivity.[27] Private industry also pays a high price. In December 1988, *Working Woman* magazine published a survey showing that almost 90 percent of the Fortune 500 companies have received sexual harassment complaints, over a third have been hit with a lawsuit, and nearly a fourth have been repeatedly sued.[28]

Surveys have consistently shown that in workplaces across the country, between 50 and 80 percent of women and 15 to 30 percent of men have experienced at least one incident meeting the definition of sexual harassment. These surveys show that the typical incident for a female involves an unmarried woman and an older, usually married, man. The typical incident reported by a man is an act by a younger, divorced or single woman or by another man. Men surveyed tend to view sexual overtures from women at work as mutual, whereas women more often view male overtures as unwelcome.[29] Harassment is, by definition, unwelcome. Women in nontraditional jobs such as coal mining report a shocking number of harassment incidents, including rape.

This kind of sexual pressure also produces an inestimable loss of productivity and damage to careers in colleges and universities. Hundreds of documented cases exist in which students have had their grades lowered, been forced to change their majors, changed colleges, or switched jobs or even fields, all because they could not stop a pattern of sexual harassment.[30] On college and university campuses, from 11 to 65 percent of female students report some form of sexual harassment, including unwanted touching, sexual remarks, or outright propositions from their professors.[31]

Students or employees may happily plan their college or work careers and then face with shocked disbelief the fact that they're being subjected to sexual blackmail. Harassment frequently causes such physical symptoms as gastrointestinal problems or severe headaches, which often require a doctor's care. Not only are nearly one-half of harassed people fired or forced to resign if they do not give in, but often they can't recover financially because they cannot get letters of recommendation or they fear telling prospective employers what happened to them.

One reason sexual harassment causes such severe stress is that—as in all sexual exploitation—the blame tends to fall on the victim. In this confused society, perpetrators may genuinely *believe* that the victim is exaggerating her complaints. Especially if the charges involve being forced to tolerate "a little good-natured teasing" or "mere" sexual comments with no propositions, other workers may call the harassed person a troublemaker. They may further harass the victim and accuse her of being oversensitive and humorless. Women are supposed to be "nice," and are somehow supposed to defend themselves without coming on strong. Femininity is equated with being passive; an assertive woman is strange and disturbing; so women are damned if they assert themselves and victimized if they don't. In the words of Voltaire, "This animal is evil; when attacked, it defends itself."

THE DEGREES
OF SEXUAL HARASSMENT

The sexual harasser often begins by testing the potential victim with looks or flirtatious comments. But some go so far as to sexually assault an employee or student with no preliminaries. There is no way to predict precisely how harassment will begin.

ASSERTIVE WAYS TO STOP
SEXUAL HARASSMENT

There is evidence that assertiveness sometimes improves the situation. But it must be done thoughtfully, and gauged to fit the level of harassment. Once again, people with high self-esteem tend to recognize disrespectful treatment and are inclined to assert themselves against harassment. You must believe that you deserve respect as a worker or student.

If you are sexually harassed, you probably want to keep your job or stay in your class. All studies show that victims (students or employers) are *very reluctant* to bring incidents to the attention of the organization. But unless they do, this offense will continue unabated. Many employers or school officials think they have no harassment problems because no one complains.

Most campuses and employers address sexual harassment complaints informally. The first step in bringing the incident to the organization's attention is *rarely* an official complaint. Experts urge that you use informal means to begin your complaint, such as going to an affirmative action director, a women's center, an ombudsperson, a human resources officer, a trusted professor, supervisor, or other mentor. Usually you will need advice from some knowledgeable person.

Although you may fantasize about telling off this abuser in no uncertain terms, realistically you need to think ahead and plan before you act, preferably with good advice from someone else. Most harassment complaints are resolved before they reach the court. Legal remedies against harassment require tremendous emotional energy and time; they result in physical as well as mental stress. Avoid them if you can.

WHAT DOES SHE MEAN?

The person who wants to prevent harassment has to do a bit of self-evaluation. As I've mentioned at several points in this book, many American men read friendly messages from women as sexual. Every group of sex offenders from obscene phone callers to acquaintance rapists shows confusion about this issue. *But misreading women's intentions shows up even in surveys of normal men.*[32] The entire culture aims to convince men that women are oversexed and always available. You can monitor how well you communicate your intention to stay in your student or professional roles when you're at school or at work.

LEARNING A NEW PROFESSIONALISM

Harassment in the workplace has been around a long time. Documented cases of sexual harassment occurred in the 18th century among housemaids in Boston and "mill girls" in Philadelphia. Today, workers have still not learned how to leave behind the old, sexist ways of behaving. Men and women need to learn new reactions to each other. It is inappropriate to tease someone about his race or his age; it is equally inappropriate to remark about someone's sexuality at work or school.

Professionally Pleasant versus Friendly

We Americans consider friendliness a desirable quality and a social advantage. Certainly we would not want our employers or professors to think us unnecessarily aloof. Good working relationships go more smoothly when everyone is pleasant. It's fun to look forward to an agreeable day at work or school.

But workers and students need to learn a precise line between a *pleasant attitude* appropriate to their role and the kind of *friendliness* that could imply sexual openness in a society like ours. You need to do a little reversal in your mind to check out your behavior. Let's say you are a heterosexual female. Do you react to your boss with the same attitude as if he were a woman? If you are a homosexual male, and you have a male employer, do you react to him with the same neutrality as if he were a female? That is, reverse the genders and test whether your behavior communicates sexual overtones:

> *Employer:* That's an *awful cute* dress you have on, Marla. (Winks)
>
> *Marla:* Gee, thanks. You like it? (She smiles, knowing it's a sexual compliment. She looks at her employer for a moment and stops work. In the view of the hopeful employer, she responds much the same as she would to a male friend or boyfriend.)

That compliment could come from a well-meaning employer, although experts nowadays advise employers to remain impersonal. Such sexual comments or gestures happen all the time. But she doesn't know what meaning her employer intends to convey. She could have responded as if her mother or a casual acquaintance had complimented her:

> *Marla:* (Pleasantly, looking up for a moment) Thanks. (Goes back to her work)

If you're concerned about how well you stay in your role, ask for some feedback from trusted friends or coworkers about the messages that you convey. Try to establish that fine line between "professionally pleasant" and "friendly." And sometimes there is a further line, and a very thin one, between "friendly" and "flirtatious" or "seductive."

Friendly versus Seductive

That line is even more difficult to draw. The comment made by Marla's employer, and the wink, were flirtatious. Of course, it's impossible to ignore someone's gender. But a lot of semi-flirtatious behavior goes on in the office or school. It can be fun, and it's harmless—as long as there's no misunderstanding of your intentions. But in the face of this serious national problem, experts advise that, when in doubt, everyone should learn how to be businesslike at work. Flirting may be harmless if the recipient interprets your meaning correctly, but are you willing to stake your job or school success on that?

THE PRESSURE TO 'SMOOTH IT OVER'

One common way a person tries to repel the advances of someone in power is to try to "smooth it over." A tiny minority of women are flattered by sexual overtures from supervisors and play along, hoping to get something out of the harasser. Most women are very uncomfortable and simply try to remain pleasant in hopes that nothing harmful will happen. Smoothing it over (by continuing to be just as friendly after the harassment) does not work very well; often the harasser regards it as a positive response or even a come-on. Remember, thousands of people distort the sexual meaning of other people's behavior in our society. So you need to be cautious about your body language. When you're trying to patch up an argument with a loved and trusted person, you can operate very differently from the actions you need to take against a sexual harasser.

GETTING YOUR PROFESSIONALISM ACROSS

These rules help people convey their businesslike intentions:

1. Evaluate your eye contact. You know what flirting is. You know how you speak to someone about business. Look the harasser in the eye, but pretend it's your banker or your physician.

2. Perfect the professional smile. Think of how you smile at a sales clerk when you are shopping, or how you smile at someone who helps you in the doctor's office. This smile is not necessarily insincere, just different. Now think of how you smile at someone to whom you're sexually attracted. A smile is often misinterpreted. Even if you're not ready to be assertive, consider very carefully before you smile immediately after an incident of harassment. If you were telling a child to stop being rude, you would not smile or the child would receive a confusing message.

3. Evaluate the sexiness or business message expressed by your clothes. You have a perfect *right* to dress in any way you want that is inside the law or company regulations. *But you are living in a society that is confused about your sexual availability.* Fashion often encourages styles that are highly exciting and seen as seductive. There may be some other kinds of clothes that you could enjoy wearing. Your message should clearly indicate that you are in a professional or a student role.

These suggestions are not intended to blame employees or students who are harassed. We have blamed victims for too long. Harassment by its very definition is *unwelcome*. However, if you worked among people who believed stealing money was okay, I'd tell you not to wear your billfold on your hip. Stealing is not right, it's not fair, and the thieves should be held responsible. But if you want to help yourself you have to recognize the sickness of your society's attitudes and try to protect yourself from being victimized by them.

HOW TO REWARD OR PUNISH THE HARASSER

Another way to stop a harasser cold as soon as the problem begins is to *reward businesslike behavior* but *not respond* to even mildly flirtatious or sexually related behavior. Watch for what Caroline rewards and punishes in a conversation with her new boss:

> *Caroline:* When did you want me to do these papers, then?
>
> *Employer:* (Grins suggestively) Maybe we could *stay late*, huh, Caroline?
>
> Caroline does not reply, but busies herself with some things on her desk. (To some harassers, this is a negative response. The implication is, "I won't respond to that.")

In a few seconds, he turns to her again.

> *Employer:* These should be done by noon tomorrow.
>
> *Caroline:* (Pleasantly) Okay. I'll get the other folders. (Her implication is, "Now you're acting appropriately and I'll respond.")

Caroline is not cool all the time. She just responds positively when she's treated in a way that is suitable for their relationship. When someone flirts or behaves in any way unbusinesslike, she doesn't answer instantly if she can delay briefly or look away, or she makes it seem that she can't believe he really did say such a thing. This pattern of response is called "shaping," and we do it all the time—it's how people learn what our limits are.

You may be able to set limits and make yourself clear at the beginning. If harassment occurs anyway, that fact does not mean it was your fault. We're talking about setting limits on an abuser just as a teacher might with a child who is too loud or too aggressive.

Students can also use this shaping technique. Let's say Professor Smith has invited Ms. Schultz into his office to discuss her paper.

> *Prof. Smith:* Cerese, this is an excellent paper. I thought you were special, and you are.
>
> *Ms. Schultz:* (Does not smile, but looks interested in his opinion about her paper) Thank you, Dr. Smith. I'm glad you thought my paper was good.
>
> *Prof. Smith:* You're quite a fascinating young lady.
>
> *Ms. Schultz:* (Ignores the last remark and returns to the only appropriate subject) Did you have any criticisms? I'd like to improve my writing style.

First, when he began to get personal, she did not smile. But she said the socially appropriate thing—what she would say in any business or professional transaction. Secondly, when he started telling her she was fascinating, she moved the conversation straight back to her school goals.

This technique involves two basic strategies:

1. Reward positive nonsexual comments, act as if they are professional, and respond professionally.

2. Ignore or defuse personal comments by remarking on the business at hand.

When the Harasser Persists

The next level of offense occurs when the harasser will not be deflected, defused, or ignored. He persists:

> *Professor:* Why do you keep ignoring me? (Takes her hand)

Here, the victim is at a decision point. She wants a good grade, a good recommendation, or a good job. Nevertheless, now she needs to be direct:

> *Marla:* (Removing her hand) I'm not ignoring you, Dr. Smith, I just don't want you to do that.
>
> Or: I'm trying to keep this a professional relationship, Dr. Smith.
>
> Or a very naive reminder: Gosh, I'm your *student*, Dr. Smith.

Suppose Mr. Jones, a high school coach, asks a student to pose in a jock-strap. (I have known these "photography" techniques to be imposed upon both males and females, by both male and female harassers.)

> *Mr. Jones:* Say, Eric, you know what might be nice? You have a great body, and it might look good to have some shots of you (opens the drawer of the desk, holds up a jockstrap) in one of these, maybe.
>
> *Eric:* (Taken by surprise, wants to give himself a moment) I'm not sure I know what you mean, Coach.
>
> *Mr. Jones:* Oh, just put on one of these and we'll take your picture, just for fun.
>
> *Eric:* Oh, no, I—I'd feel very uncomfortable doing that.
>
> Or: That's not for me.

Note that he makes an I-statement. A potential victim may not be able to think of anything to say to a proposition, but you can always fall back on the good old I-statement, *"I'd feel very uncomfortable doing that."* You could say the same thing when your professor or employer invites you somewhere inappropriate to your role, or when any suggestion is made which results in your feeling ill at ease.

A common tactic used by a professor or employer is to ask very personal questions. Let's imagine that you were not prepared the first time this happened, and you've already answered a few questions that seemed unsuitable. After reading this, you decide you are going to draw the lines of your role more carefully. You could handle it like this:

> *Professor:* What do you and your boyfriend do? Are you...intimate with him?
>
> *You:* Wow, I'd feel very uncomfortable sharing that with one of my *teachers*.
>
> *Professor:* What for? I care about you.
>
> *You:* Could I ask you to explain that exam question from yesterday?

This student is sticking to business. She's ignoring the sexual overtones to see whether the professor will give up.

Learn to change the subject. Some hard-core harassers won't allow it, but you can often fend off a tentative harasser with these kinds of remarks. Of course, it takes experience sometimes to be able to banter easily. Practice in front of the mirror. Ask a friend to role-play it with you: "You be Professor Smith and I'll..."

COWORKER HARASSMENT

Employers are legally liable if their employees are sexually harassed by their coworkers. What if a coworker continually makes sexual remarks and you're embarrassed and angry about it? This kind of teasing often falls into the illegal category despite the fact that the person in power is not directly involved:

> *Coworker:* Why don't you just lean over his desk and give him a good look? That'll make him give you a raise.
>
> *Sheryl:* Joe, I am getting really sick of your sexual remarks. This is a *professional* relationship, and sex has no place in it.

MAKING A JOKE

It's difficult for most people to think of a joke as a response to harassment, but some people are artists at turning an insult into a joke. For example, Elissa Clarke tells of a steel worker whose male coworkers howled like dogs when women first showed up on the job. So she brought a box of dog biscuits and tossed one at the men every time they howled.[33]

You might find a way to joke that stops harassment. But you need to be aware that the harasser may already think it's a joke. If you ever decide to make an official complaint, you will need to demonstrate that from the very beginning, *you did not like the harassment.* So if you're good at joking turn-offs, consider using them only for low-level harassment. If the harassment doesn't stop, the joke may be encouraging it.

AVOID BEING ALONE WITH THE HARASSER

Try to avoid being alone with people who are giving you any of the signals of beginning harassment. If a harasser maneuvers you to be alone with him, you could say:

> *You:* I can't stop by your office today—I'll pick it up after your lecture.
>
> Or: Sorry, I can't stay late—have to leave on time today.

KEEPING A RECORD

If you experience even one episode of harassment, you should keep a written record of all harassing incidents, and of any complaints you lodge against the harasser, school, or company. For each instance, make a complete record:

1. Where the incident occurred.
2. The date and time of occurrence.
3. What happened.
4. What was said.
5. How you felt.
6. The names of any witnesses or others who have been harassed by this person or at this company or institution.

You may also want to consider two additional steps. Employees have access to their files in a few states. You may want to check your personnel file, and keep copies of positive evaluations if you can. Better yet, get a copy of good evaluations when they are given and keep them for your future use. Sometimes they are removed in retaliation for your resisting sexual harassment.

Some authors suggest that you carry a hidden tape recorder into any discussions with someone who has sexually harassed you. A tape recording made in this manner probably is inadmissible in a court of law. But its legal use is not the reason why someone would carry a hidden recorder. It can back up an informal complaint or a formal complaint that stays within the organization or grievance process. One expert on sexual harassment advises that if you've got the goods on the harasser, the company will be far more interested in settling the complaint.[34] A playback of such a recording to a campus or company ombudsperson could have a *powerful* effect and could get action fast on informal resolution. For example, the harasser could be seriously disciplined. Carrying a hidden recorder may be illegal in a few states; you need to check that out first.

ARRANGING A TALK

Suppose you have tried everything you know outside of complaining directly to the harasser or higher-ups. To your disappointment, the harassment continues. You could arrange a talk and tell the offender your reactions and what you want.

For example, let's say Lou works under the supervision of Joanne, who has repeatedly tried to get him alone where she rubs up against him and tries to kiss him. Lately, since he's avoided all of these situations, she's been assigning him an impossible amount of extra work and behaving in a rude and hostile manner. Lou feels he just can't go on like this. This job is very important to him. He makes an appointment to talk with her.

> *Lou:* Joanne, you know, I'm really worried about something, and I need to tell you. Over the last few weeks when you've tried to kiss me and touch me, I haven't responded. Now I notice you've been giving me more work and acting really angry at me. (Here he describes what happened.) This has me so worried that I have not slept at night more than a few hours for weeks. I've even had some medical problems. (Here he describes the effect the harassment is having on him.)
>
> *Joanne:* (Interrupts) You're imagining things, Lou.
>
> *Lou:* Well, I want to tell you how it seems to me. I want you to stop trying to kiss me or touch me. I want to

be able to do my job and have a good working relationship with everybody here. (Here he says what he
wants to happen.) I think you and I can have a good
working relationship.

Talks like this may stop the problem before it goes further.
One advantage of a talk is that it's still less formal than the next
steps you could take. One disadvantage is, there's no record of the
conversation unless you tape record it. It will probably not seem
as official as a letter, but that could be a benefit as well.

WRITING A LETTER

Another method of dealing with harassment is the idea of Mary
Rowe, an assistant to the president of the Massachusetts Institute
of Technology.[35] This technique involves writing a letter to the
harasser. Before you do this, try to get the advice of a trusted and
experienced person, often a campus ombudsperson or director of
the women's center. Rowe advises that the letter include the same
three parts as the personal talk above:

1. Describe what happened:

   "You've asked me out four times."

   "You keep mentioning sex with me."

   "You've made jokes about my body."

2. Describe how you feel:

   "My stomach is in knots all day."

   "I can't sleep over this."

   "Since then I've had constant headaches."

   "I'm so humiliated I want to hide."

3. Describe what you would like to happen:

   "I want to be strictly professional."

   "I want you to stop making any sexual remarks to me."

   "I want you to treat me like a student."

This action results in some advantages: you have a record, you have taken your own power rather than feeling helpless, and you have proof that you made an active effort to stop the harassment. It is best, Rowe advises, if someone accompanies you when you deliver the letter.

But there are also some disadvantages in the letter-writing technique. Lois Vander Waerdt, an attorney and sexual harassment expert, advises that such a letter lets the institution off the hook and makes the victim responsible for solving the problem herself. The letter could also limit a plaintiff's court case. "If the institutional grapevine gives good marks to the campus or company for resolving these matters, complaining through their channels is a much more effective means of addressing sexual harassment and getting it stopped."[36] Vander Waerdt points out that harassers usually approach several targets; writing a letter only to the harasser won't help anyone else whom the harasser approaches, and it does not let the organization know about the harassment.

SEEKING EMOTIONAL SUPPORT

If you are the victim of sexual harassment you need someone to talk to besides the official who receives your complaint; it's important for you to get support from people you trust with the whole story, where you can express all your feelings. It's a shock and a terrific burden to face injustice on a daily basis. But in your anger and fright, do not go spreading accusations around indiscriminately, or you may be accused of slander. Talk to professionals or trusted people. In confiding, you may also find others whose ordeals corroborate your own. Most harassers approach more than one person, and have a "modus operandi," or typical pattern. Networking with other victims can give you important information and strengthen your case.

OTHER OPTIONS BEFORE TAKING LEGAL ACTION

You may go to your supervisor, your advisor or counselor, or your union representative with this problem if you have not been able to resolve it at lower levels. The appropriate person on a campus could be called an "ombudsperson" or a "designated sexual harassment advisor." Most colleges and universities have specified people to whom you can complain, and who know the grievance procedures for sexual harassment.

The law requires the company or campus to *act reasonably*. This duty may mean taking action without your permission, and "reasonably" may mean keeping your identity confidential. When you complain, ask about these two things. Take your documentation with you. Again, stress the three points: this is what happened, this is how I'm feeling, this is what I want to happen.

LEGAL REMEDIES

Despite the anguish that sexual harassment causes, we have made progress. At long last, all forms of sexual harassment are illegal. Title IX prohibits discrimination in education at any institution receiving federal funds. Title VII of the Civil Rights Act of 1964 prohibits discrimination in employment on the basis of race, color, religion, national origin, and sex.

But this is not to say that legal action is easy or that it will be the best thing for you. As with rape, the victim may have to undergo distressing mistreatment. See Appendix for a chart of legal remedies against sexual harassment.

PREVENTION OF FURTHER HARASSMENT

In order to set up a work situation free from harassment, employers or schools are *required* to take specific steps:

1. Publicize the laws forbidding harassment at work and school.
2. Train supervisors and other staff to increase their awareness of what constitutes harassment.
3. Set up grievance procedures so that anyone being harassed can make a complaint within the organization.

UNETHICAL 'HELPING' PROFESSIONALS

There is a kind of sexual harassment that may be legal but which violates the codes of ethics in the helping professions. In all but the rarest of cases, this harassment leaves the victim even more wounded than when she sought help. Its perpetrators, who are therapists, clergymen, physicians, and other professionals, make sexual advances toward patients or clients to such an extent that thousands are still trying to recover from the damage. While men are occasionally abused in this way, again the victims are overwhelmingly female. This kind of exploitation is so common that ethics committees in the helping professions are under extreme pressure to review their guidelines.

Peter Rutter, M.D., exposes the extent of this epidemic in his book *Sex in the Forbidden Zone*. Rutter talks about the confusion of sex with power in our society and the sexual sickness that encourages this attitude in all of us. Many women think at first that their situation is different ("My therapist is not abusive, he loves me"). But after interviewing hundreds of victims from all walks of life, Rutter is convinced that this behavior constitutes a serious form of abuse. He defines sex in the forbidden zone:

> *Sexual behavior between a man and a woman who have a professional relationship based on trust, specifically when the man is the woman's doctor, psychotherapist, pastor, lawyer, teacher, or workplace mentor.*[37]

Once again, the dysfunctional attitudes of society encourage both the professional *and* the victim to become involved when sexual feelings arise. The whole culture encourages men to challenge women's intimate boundaries. Rutter believes that our society discourages men from learning to empathize with women. He laments this loss for men as well, because "they have so much more to offer women than predatory sexual opportunism."

But society also programs women to respond positively to men in power, to feel tremendously flattered by the advances of a male professional. Many women, pondering the months and years required for them to recover from this exploitation, say they were almost in a trance at the time. Even if the man physically repelled them, they felt they could do nothing but go along. Some even recognized that they were initiating a sexual relationship in order to repeat seductive patterns of their childhood.

We hold adults responsible for sexually exploiting children; we have to hold professionals responsible for exploiting vulnerable adults, for not maintaining their professional ethics. In the overwhelming majority of cases, survivors claim that the experience reaped bitter consequences ranging from the inability to complete psychotherapy to the failure to obtain an adequate divorce settlement because of retaliation from attorneys who were their former lovers. They frequently mourn the fact that they have been unable to form another relationship for years afterward without seeking out the role of victim.

In the most common professional exploitation, seduction—not force—is involved. The question the woman needs to ask is not, "What can I *say* to respond to such a dilemma?" The issue is, "How can I get hold of my *feelings* in order to see clearly that I am dealing with an exploiter?" What should you do if you're faced with professional abuse?

Mental health professionals: social workers, psychiatrists, counselors, psychologists

Cassie, a woman twenty years old, has been consulting a psychologist for several years. He's never seduced her. In fact, he merely kisses her on the cheek when she arrives and when she leaves, and asks her about her sex life. (In his precise words, "Who have you f---ed lately?") She did not think that this behavior was a big deal, but she was not getting better. A friend urged her to find another therapist, but she said her parents liked the psychologist and wouldn't pay for anyone else.

I once asked a reputable psychiatrist what he thought a patient should say if a therapist suggested anything sexual. He replied, "Goodbye." If a mental health professional gives you *any* sexual attention, whether it makes you uncomfortable or not, it is a serious violation of that person's professional ethics. Many of us believe that therapists who attempt intercourse with their patients, *with their consent or not,* should be tried for rape. Many mentally ill women have remained untreated for years because a lack of trust resulted from this kind of abuse. In the depression that may follow the sudden realization that they have been used, a number of women commit suicide.

There *is* no excuse, there *is* no possible reason for such sexual attention. All the rationalizations a therapist may offer are completely self-serving. A therapist says this is part of treatment? If sex is so therapeutic, why doesn't he offer this kind of therapy to everyone regardless of age or sexual attractiveness? He is exploiting his client, who should leave at once and call one of the resources in the Appendix to find a new therapist. Emotional support is available from a local crisis hotline, counseling center, or women's group, which can offer perspective (even men victims should try these numbers for a referral). Local professional associations can help determine where to file a complaint. A therapist's title or status is no reason for awe—he is no more than an abuser with a degree.

Physicians, nurses, dentists, and other medical professionals

It is unethical for any person who is treating you medically to give you sexual attention of any kind. Such attention can put you in the difficult position that, if either of you changes your mind, you may be rejected and, in retaliation, denied competent medical care. All sorts of possibilities arise when you mix sex with a professional relationship. However attractive your physician might be, however strong your need for fantasy and love, you're taking a big chance if you willingly become involved. Such liaisons almost never develop into healthy and lasting relationships, and it is almost always the one without power who does the suffering.

The sexual harasser sometimes knows just how far to go for gratification without getting into trouble. In the case of Jody, for example, her dentist brushed up against her breasts on three occasions. Not knowing what to do, she just changed dentists. But for years she questioned herself—had she been accurate? Was it just an accident? Or had she done something to encourage him? Every time she thought about the experience, she felt so ashamed and embarrassed that she told no one until years later.

Sometimes we are under extreme pressure not to offend a medical professional. I remember when my fourteen-year-old child lay in the hospital with a fractured skull. The first time I spoke to the neurosurgeon, I did not like his arrogant attitude. He would not give me information, since he had all the answers. Had he not been the doctor on call during this emergency, I would never have chosen him. But I instantly heard a little voice inside warning me to be careful not to offend him; wasn't my child's life in his hands? How could I possibly change doctors quickly enough not to hurt her treatment? Would I be branded with the reputation of a troublemaker by switching, so that no other doctor would take on the case? Fortunately, this arrogance was not so offensive that I couldn't tolerate it. How much more pressure might a person feel in a life-and-death situation when sexual overtures are made?

In such a predicament, an excuse can be a turn-off:

> "I'm just so worried. Could we get back to the treatment plan?"

Or perhaps the overture has to be confronted with the good old, all-purpose I-statement:

> "Dr. Adams, I feel really uncomfortable when you do that. Please stop."

The above option is for times when the attention is unwelcome and you feel you cannot switch to another doctor. It is the ultimate cruelty for anyone you're depending upon to proposition you sexually during the stress of a crisis. Some exploiters have even waited until a patient was desperate or even suicidal before making a seductive move. If you are in a situation where you can immediately get help elsewhere, this would be the wisest course of action. The seducer knows what he is doing. He is like a predatory animal lurking near wounded prey: he knows you are vulnerable.

Attorneys

Any professional relationship is better off uncontaminated by extra kinds of emotional baggage. What if you have an affair with your attorney and your relationship sours before you go to court? What if the attorney thinks his first bill was unduly low and revises it upward? If you argue, will he begin to identify with your estranged spouse's cause? As needy as human beings can be, they should watch out for any situations that mix personal with professional roles. *You* may be able to handle such mixing, but if the other person cannot, trouble could result.

TREATMENT FOR SEXUAL HARASSERS

Harassers may be helped by counseling or groups for sexual addicts. See Appendix for resources.

ASSERTIVENESS ON TAP

The assertive attitude does not always have to be put into words, but it can be there for you to draw upon. If you are aware of your rights and you think you're worth it, even your body language tends to convey your intention to stay within your role as a student, employee, parishioner, or client. More potential harassers will notice, and it will be more difficult for the potential abuser to fantasize about your being passively cooperative.

CHAPTER SEVEN

Avoiding Acquaintance Rape

what can we do there is no one else
to protect us
but ourselves[38]

—dell fitzgerald-richards

An impressive number of surveyors has attempted to estimate the rate of rape in the United States. Averaging the findings of all those studies, experts judge that the chances of an American woman being raped in her lifetime are one in four. The odds are about one in three that she will be the target of either an actual or an *attempted* rape. The Senate Judiciary Committee recently released statistics showing that every hour, sixteen women confront rapists. The rate of rape in the United States is more than twenty times that of Japan and thirteen times that of Britain.[39]

Legal definitions of rape vary from state to state, but the language everywhere includes penile penetration of the vagina by physical force or under threat of physical harm. State laws differ on whether rape includes male victims, oral or anal sex, or intercourse with an intoxicated person who is unable to resist. Often where an action is not legally considered to be rape, it constitutes sexual assault: for example, forcible penetration of the vagina or anus with an object such as a bottle or broom handle. Statutory rape refers to intercourse with a person under the age of consent, regardless of the willingness of the victim. In some states it is legal for a man to force sex upon his wife; it is not rape. These barbaric laws permitting marital rape are gradually being changed as test cases come to court in individual states.

RAPE-FREE SOCIETIES

Rape is not a part of human nature; it is an act found largely in violent cultures. In fact, there are societies in which rape is either absent or rare. Peggy Sanday, an anthropologist, studied over 156 societies. In rape-free cultures, she found, women participate in religion, politics, or economics as freely as men do. It is also characteristic that relationships among people and groups are nonviolent, as opposed to the violence of the rape-prone societies.[40]

THE CULTURE OF RAPE

Once your consciousness is raised about the way our society encourages rape, you may feel yourself to be a misfit. In a way, you are. Study after study indicates that we are a particularly rape-prone society. One of the symptoms of a rape-prone society is that, when someone becomes alarmed about it, she seems somehow to be a far-out, overly sensitive person who is making a mountain out of a molehill. The rape-prone attitudes are so ingrained that even nonviolent Americans have distorted opinions on the subject.

Rape can be committed against any person, whether young or old, rich or poor, male or female, black, white, yellow, or brown. Although some rape survivors escape damage, rape can cause serious psychological trauma to both female and male victims. Virtually all male victims are raped (penetrated anally or orally) by men; a very few cases (not even expressible in a fraction of a percent) of men are raped by women. It is possible for males to become sexually aroused without wanting to have intercourse; in rare instances, a man has been tied down and tortured, sometimes for hours, while one or more women had intercourse with him. Some of these men have required extensive sex therapy to overcome the dysfunctions that resulted from these experiences. It helps men to feel empathy with rape victims if they realize that rape is a violation that can happen to anyone.

While examples in this chapter may seem more pertinent to women, such events affect men in indirect but powerful ways. The rape of one woman generates fear in other women. This fear also injures innocent men because they themselves provoke fear. In addition to the fact that males can be rape victims, they suffer from living in a society where half the population has reason to be resentful, suspicious, and scared.

People who have not been through the experience often do not understand the rape victim's feelings. The emotions associated with being physically violated are difficult to comprehend, particularly when a male has been socialized to think that "getting a piece" is always hilarious good fun. After all, doesn't everyone want to "get a little"? Here is a rape survivor's description of how she felt a month after a date raped her and forced her to have oral sex:

> I cut off all my hair. I did not want to be attractive to men. I started wearing real androgynous clothes—nothing tight, nothing revealing—and reduced my makeup to almost nil. I just wanted to look neutered for a while because that felt safer.[41]

This woman did not date again for several years. Both men and women survivors of rape report a variety of reactions, most of which involve fear and loss of self-esteem. They often need counseling to help them adjust. Rape does not invariably cause psychological damage. But if you experience any negative changes in your life after a rape, such as depression or excessive fears, even if they seem unrelated to the incident, you may want to check it out with a counselor (see Appendix pp. 240–241).

Victims and Survivors

Workers in the field of sexuality prefer to use the term "survivor" in place of "victim" whenever possible. The word "survivor" emphasizes prevailing over the experience. When I am discussing ways to avoid being victimized, I may use the word "victim." But "survivor" is a word that can make a profound difference when applied to oneself. I recall a quotation from some unnamed source: "Life is the transcendence of loss." I would rephrase it to say that *"Successful* life is the transcendence of loss." The person who is victimized loses a feeling of safety in this world. Some of that loss can be reclaimed. But all of life involves losing and overcoming—losing friends, losing a love relationship, losing a chance or an opportunity. We can overcome loss and become survivors.

How the Media Influence the Rape Culture

We are socialized to believe that men scare women, but not the reverse. This training is the reason unusual movies with violent *women* scaring men, like *Fatal Attraction* and *Play Misty for Me*, are so frightening—they contradict the script that Hollywood has used for fifty years to earn so many millions of our dollars.

I cannot remember when, as a child, I first saw a film about a scared helpless woman trying to escape from a horrible crazy man who might do (who knows what?) to her. Even Dracula stalked terrified, screaming women to commit the clearly Freudian deed of sinking his teeth into their necks. I could not fathom the fact that the bad man scaring the poor, weak woman was merely an attitude of fiction. This drama seemed like reality to me. Of *course*, learns the child in America, women are scared and men are the bad guys.

Today such plots are far more frequent. Notice the pictures of brutal, vicious men and helpless women on the front of some VCR tapes in your video store. The sexual script is clear: it's exciting to see men chase helpless women, especially with sex on their minds. Children don't know that's just fiction—they decide that's how life *is*. They absorb the myths of how men and women are supposed to act.

Media dramas and novels subtly weave rape into plots; often they actually romanticize it. Even in the early seventies, force was used in about one-third of the sex scenes in hard-core paperback books, almost always by a male to coerce a female into sex against her will.[42] Recent storylines employ force much more often, and blatant pictures of coercion are common even on magazine covers. Bondage and domination increased between 1970 and 1981 to 17.2 percent of the magazine covers of heterosexual pornographic magazines.[43] Such statistics about pornography may not be surprising, but inside the covers of mainstream novels, scenes of rape and near-rape also abound.

A typical "love" scene occurs in Fred M. Stewart's novel, *Century*, where a man attempts to rape a woman in a taxi. At first she fights him off, but the reader watches her thoughts immediately afterwards as she begins to relish the idea of sexual force:

> Then she turned back to the window, hating herself for giving in to what she knew was the most primitive part of her personality. But, also, unfortunately, the most powerful....[44]

When she gives in, the reader is not surprised; that's our national script. Countless novels contain "romantic" rapes where the woman forgives the rapist, thereby reinforcing the all-American theme that women really like it.

Even Scarlett O'Hara was raped by Rhett Butler in perhaps our best-known film, *Gone With the Wind*. And she loved it, which further confuses viewers. Watching *Dangerous Liaisons* or *Doctor Zhivago*, few moviegoers realized that in each film, a young teenager was raped. But soon after the sexual coercion, each girl began to like sex and wait for the man's secret visits. Viewers forgot that they had seen a rape, so seductively did these young maidens smile over their newfound sexuality. This portrayal of females loving sexual force is one of the most dangerous ways to depict rape. Research shows that it changes the attitudes of even nonviolent men to the point that they aren't as shocked by rape and more often think women like it.[45]

In a rape-prone culture like ours, it's easy for these things to go right over your head. Rape is an intrusion into the most private part of the self—too personal to mention to any but the most trusted others. Rape survivors, like people who have been infected with sexually transmitted diseases, rarely feel comfortable talking about it. You don't know how many people around you have suffered from the experience. You could easily assume that the unmentionable is therefore not a problem. Your society propagandizes you to view rape as a rare attack by a crazed stranger. But it has happened to someone on your street, in your class, or at your workplace.

HOW CAN RAPE BE SO COMMON?

Few Americans can truly integrate the fact that rape happens to one of four American women. In an extensive, well-controlled study of over 6,000 college students, Mary Koss and others came up with the finding that 25 percent of college women have either suffered rape or attempted rape *between the ages of fourteen and twenty-one.*[46] Fifteen percent of the sample were actually raped. One in twelve men in her survey admitted to acts that meet legal definitions of rape. Remember, this was a far-reaching and comprehensive survey sampling students from a variety of schools in all sections of the United States. The reason the mind rejects these findings, which occur over and over in other studies, is that we think of rapists as sex-crazed madmen who spring from the darkness onto strangers.

But most rape is committed by someone known to the victim. Nearly all teenage victims know their attackers. By far the majority of reported rapes on college campuses are committed by fraternity members. During one recent year, two midwestern universities reported serious acquaintance rape problems—typical of large universities. On one campus 400 acquaintance rapes had been reported during the year; 75 percent were committed by fraternity men on that campus.[47] The other university reported that one of every six of its women students had been sexually assaulted during their stay at the university, and fraternity members were involved in three-fifths of these assaults.[48] These statistics are reflected in crime data from numerous other campuses. A fraternity house is one of the few places in this country where admiration of alcohol and sexual prowess combine with permission to engage in impulsive behaviors in a basically unsupervised environment. Hopefully, the efforts of fraternities to improve these conditions will have an impact on the safety of college women.

It can't be so, you say. Where did these universities obtain such findings? Were their samples biased? The answer is relatively simple: most people do not report rape. Only 5 percent of rape victims are believed to report the incident to the police. And most Americans do not realize that *all* forced sex is rape. The Koss study found that *only 27 percent of the women raped identified themselves as rape victims.* They often suffered from fear, anger, and other possible aftereffects of rape, but they were as confused as the rest of society about the definition of rape. They usually blamed themselves for what happened. When counselors encouraged some of the survivors to label their experience as an actual rape, they usually felt better. How does rape by an acquaintance actually happen? Here's Wendy's story:

> I used to go out with this guy for a while, and then we stopped seeing each other. I was not that serious. Then one day there was a knock at my door, and it was him. He said he just wanted to talk. I didn't think anything; I let him in. He started kissing me. I told him to stop. I pushed him away. He kept on. He said, "You know you love it." I said, "No I don't. Stop it!" But he kept on. He pushed me down on the bed. I kept trying, but I couldn't...I couldn't get him to stop. He...raped me. All the time he kept telling me how much I wanted it. He even saw me the next day and he said, "That wasn't rape." And I said, "Oh, yes it was." But he didn't even listen to me, he had made up his mind. He thought I loved it. I...haven't gone out with anyone since. I stay home a lot.

Rape Attitude Checklist

Acquaintance rapists *seem* to be regular guys. Their beliefs at first glance don't seem rape-prone. What are your beliefs about rape? Check true or false:

1.___Rape is a part of male nature going back to the cavemen.

2.___If a woman goes back on an agreement to have sex and the man forces her, it is not rape.

3.___All women have a secret desire to be raped.

4.___Women say "No" when they really mean "Yes."

5.___A woman frequently causes her own rape by entering a vulnerable situation, such as entering a high-crime neighborhood or a bar.

6.___It is up to the woman to keep things under control.

7.___A woman who has had sex with a man willingly, and later is forced into intercourse with that same man, has not really been raped.

8.___Rapists always physically damage the woman in some way that would show up on her body later as bruises or other signs.

9.___Masculine men naturally make sexual conquests whenever they get a chance.

10.__A woman who leads a man on deserves what she gets.

11.__Get a woman drunk or high, and she'll let a man go as far as he wants.

12.__Women attract rape by dressing seductively.

Did you mark any of the above as "True"? All of these state-ments are *myths* about rape, but they are common beliefs in our country. Rape is no more a part of male nature than baby-killing is a part of female nature. While some men and women fantasize about being raped, fantasies are under their control; no one actual-ly *desires* to be raped—which represents a total *lack* of control. Rape survivors said "No" and meant it, and the acquaintance rapist often did not believe them. Women who mean "No" certainly attempt to communicate that message to the rapist, but he either does not care or does not interpret her refusal as a true rejection.

Such is our victim-blaming mentality that, if a rapist did not leap out of the darkness, it must be the woman's fault. After all, she used to date him, or she shouldn't have stayed behind at the party, or she shouldn't have had those two drinks or worn that sweater. But if she knew him and particularly if she's been kissing and petting with him, then if he forces her...that isn't rape, is it?

Yes, it is. If she says no and tries to stop him, it is rape.

Society and even the criminal justice system often blame women for "causing" their own rape by entering vulnerable situations. Yes, hitchhikers and women who go into other dangerous situations may be raped. *But rape educators point out that just being ignorant or naive is not a rapable offense.* Many women are raped trying to get to or from work. Rape happens in suburban as well as urban areas, and not always in a place thought to be dangerous.

Studies of men who have committed rape show that they believe most of the above myths and think it is normal for sex and aggression to be mixed up together. There have been several surveys of men who rate themselves "likely to rape" if they could get by with it.[49] Repeatedly these men have said they believe the rape myths and they show a callous attitude toward rape. Many men also misread women's signals consistently, and there is plenty of research to back up this fact.[50] If she squeezes his hand in the movie, doesn't she want what he wants? This kind of misunderstanding is very frequent in male-female relationships today. Women must become aware of what men see as intentionally seductive, regardless of whether they intend it to be. If society does not make changes fast enough to make a safe environment for *you*, you will be wise to make some accommodations.

The rapist may be morally and psychologically abnormal, but statistically he is not. That is, rape-prone attitudes are so common in our society that *they* may be the norm. Scientist Neil Malamuth reported that 35 percent of the college men he interviewed said they would force sex onto a woman if they were guaranteed they could get away with it.[51] These same results show up in surveys of teenage and adult males throughout our society.

After all, is recovering from rape such a big deal? Just talk to a man who loves a rape survivor, whose beloved may have so much difficulty trusting him that their relationship cannot grow. Talk to survivors who have needed counseling, who have been afraid to go out, and who have not been able to trust men. A country that tells all its men to "score" with women cannot be expected to believe that its women really mind forced sex all that much. Aren't the victims just scoring, too? One study of college males found 83 percent agreeing to the following statement: "Some women look like they're just asking to be raped."[52] While certain clothing styles may seem seductive, don't forget: in some societies, women can walk around bare from the waist up and not get raped. The idea that anyone is asking to be *raped* because of her clothes is completely ludicrous; that she is asking for consenting sex may not even be accurate. Where respect for individual rights is strong, rape does not occur regardless of what women wear.

A sexually frustrated male can hardly be expected to control himself, can he? That's another one of the myths. Rape is not primarily a sexual act. Most stranger rapists have sexual access to girlfriends or wives. Rape is a crime of violence. Ask any incarcerated rapist and he will tell you that anger and power, not lust, were his reasons. What do acquaintance rapists report as the main feeling they had during the act?

Pride.

The suggestions in this chapter apply largely to rape by someone known to the victim—*acquaintance* rape. While sexual assertiveness is possible against stranger rapists, it obviously has more potential for preventing acquaintance rape. Most acquaintance rapes happen in the rapist's territory—his apartment, for example. The time has come to treat a stranger who wants to date you as an unknown quantity. Yet we are socialized to trust people we date. And a major problem is simply our definition of "knowing" someone. You can be acquainted with someone whom you do not *know* well enough to be alone with him.

HOW TO RECOGNIZE A POTENTIAL RAPIST

Robin Warshaw, author of *I Never Called It Rape*, offers convincing advice on how to avoid acquaintance rape, based on the experience of rape counselors and rape survivors.[53] She suggests that you learn to recognize the behaviors common to the potential rapist. Do not be surprised if you've seen these behaviors fairly often. Research clearly shows them to be present in rape- and abuse-prone personalities. Warshaw advises, that you *run, do not walk, from any man who displays any of these characteristics*:

1. *Emotionally abuses you** through insults, belittling comments, ignoring your opinion, or by acting sulky or angry when you initiate an action or idea.

2. *Tells you* who you may be friends with, how you should dress, or tries to control other elements of your life or relationship. He insists on picking the movie you'll see, the restaurant where you'll eat, and so on.

3. *Talks negatively about women* in general.

4. *Gets jealous* when there's no reason.

5. *Drinks heavily or uses drugs* and tries to get you intoxicated.

6. *Berates you* for not wanting to get drunk, get high, have sex, or go with him to an isolated personal place such as his room, your apartment, or the like.

7. *Refuses to let you share* any of the expenses of a date and gets angry if you offer to pay.

8. *Is physically violent* to you or others, even if it's 'just' grabbing and pushing to get his way.

9. *Acts in an intimidating way* toward you: sits too close, uses his body to block your way, speaks as if he knows you much better than he does, touches you when you tell him not to.

10. *Is unable to handle* sexual and emotional frustrations without becoming angry.

11. *Doesn't view you as an equal,* either because he's older or because he sees himself as smarter or socially superior.

12. *Has a fascination with weapons.*

13. *Enjoys being cruel* to animals, children, or people he can bully.

---

* Italics are mine.

If you find that you repeatedly become involved with men who have any of these characteristics, you must consider why you *choose* this kind of person. After a few times, it is not just chance. A person with self-esteem does not stick around to be demeaned and frightened. Find yourself a good support group, or go to a therapist or counselor to help yourself understand this self-destructive behavior. You may want to read some books about addictive relationships. One example is *Men Who Hate Women and the Women Who Love Them.*[54]

TALKING TO THE POTENTIAL RAPIST

It is far better to ignore and steer clear of such men as Warshaw describes above. The major distortion in the minds of most acquaintance rapists is their tendency to interpret friendliness as seduction. She may be refusing him, but she won't be able to get her resistance across. This misunderstanding of a woman's intentions is even present in many nonrapists, because the entire culture encourages it. Look for Warshaw's clues early and get yourself out of the situation. Don't be challenged by wanting to "shape this guy up" with your assertiveness. *He does not perceive reality the way you do.* Don't hold on to the hope that, because he's so good-looking or so popular, you can bring out his decent inner nature if you're just nice to him. When you act "nice" toward him, especially if you've tolerated *any* put-downs such as outlined above, you are signaling to him that you are fair game for more.

However, you may find you are in a situation you feel you cannot leave. If you want to establish yourself as unavailable, then assertive responses can help you get that across.

When Someone Tries to Get You Drunk

Let's say that you attend a party at a friend's house, and a nice-looking guy keeps making eye contact with you. At first you are interested. But after listening to him awhile, you note that he drops a few remarks about stupid women and is trying to get you to drink more than you want. You've tried walking to the other side of the room, but he follows you. He begins to engage the other people in your group in conversation about you:

> *He:* This little gal here, she's just a party pooper, she won't take any of this good stuff (pushes a bottle at you and grins).

You: I *don't want* any. (You turn and walk away.)

Never smile at the joke. He may be one of the millions who misinterpret a smile as a come-on. You're not pleased—you must be totally clear.

When Someone Gets Too Close Physically

Some men are sensitive to mild assertion such as your continually scooting away. The next level of assertiveness is to say, "Please stop sitting so close."

If that doesn't stop him, rape counselors advise that you escalate: leave, push him away, or tell him, "Get off!" He's already showing insensitivity to your rights. A considerate man who wants to impress you starts with conversation, not with physically pushing you.

Suppose a man in whom you are not interested puts his arm around your waist although you move away and otherwise resist. Rape prevention experts recommend that you speak sharply:

"Stop that!"

If he does not stop, they advise you to escalate:

"Stop that! Take your hands off me!"

That's not nice, and that's not sweet—why, that sounds like some kind of far-out women's libber, no doubt. If you repel this intruder, someone might say you weren't *polite*. Or someone might not even *like* you. Or even call you a *bitch*, heaven forbid. Keep your priorities straight. The experts advise: *better rude than raped!* If you are uncomfortable defending your sexual boundaries, it is not that this advice is too strong. It's that you're among the brainwashed. You've bought the cultural myths about assertive women being aggressive. *The highest rates of acquaintance rape occur to inexperienced and naive young women who were trying to be "nice."* Any rape education expert at a college will tell you the biggest challenge in working with women: helping them to feel comfortable taking their own power.

It is not unfeminine to have self-esteem. It is feminine to defend yourself. It is feminine to have courage. Your pioneer or

Native American ancestors, your slave ancestors, or your immigrant ancestors were strong women. Feel them there with you inside your mind. You need to be furious with anyone who violates your boundaries. You need to feel, "How dare you!"

When a Date Is Excessively Jealous

How can you answer a date who shows excessive jealousy? Be very alert to any kinds of jealous remarks:

> *He:* Why the hell are you talking to *him*, when you came with *me?*

Don't start defending yourself. There's no point in trying to reassure a person with such distorted attitudes. If your date talks like this, don't even risk going home with him. Try to get a ride with someone you trust. It is *not* normal to restrict a date from even talking to another person. That's the red flag of an abuser waving in your face.

These are not relationships you should work to improve, but non-relationships, and you want to make that crystal clear. These men are showing signs of being sexual intruders and may be more dangerous than an obscene phone caller or an exhibitionist. Don't smile, don't engage in polite conversation as if the man had not said or done something on Warshaw's list. You may find yourself confused because these attitudes are so common in men—but so is rape.

When Someone Uses Words or Names That Are Too Familiar

What if someone calls you names you're not comfortable with, or acts as if he knows you better than he does? Get away from him. If you can't do that quickly, respond clearly:

> *"Stop calling me that. I don't like it."*
>
> *"You don't know me. Leave me alone."*

Suppose a man continues to put you down and tries to establish himself as your social superior. This kind of comment is common in acquaintance rapists:

He: (Teasing) You don't know what you're talking about. That's stupid. (He tweaks your hair and grins down at you.)

You: (Over your shoulder as you walk away) I don't like to be teased, and I don't like to be called names. (No smile)

Doesn't that sound downright unfriendly? It's not nice to talk tough. But this is a situation that threatens you. It does not call for niceness. You can be nice, too, where it's appropriate. You can still keep "nice" for other times.

The Shock Technique: Call It What It Is

If you are with someone who is trying to force you to have sexual intercourse or oral sex, or keeps acting like he thinks you "want it" although you're saying no, you could say:

"This is rape! I'm calling the police!"

With the kinds of distortions this man has been making, he may need to have his behavior clarified. Another reality jolt is:

"Did you know that what you are doing is a felony? You could go to prison for this!"

RULES FOR AVOIDING ACQUAINTANCE RAPE

In addition, consider the following suggestions from acquaintance rape survivors. The advice also applies to gay males, who are raped at an astonishingly high rate in some places:

1. *Set sexual limits and communicate them to your date.* Chapters 4 and 5 show you how to make a policy statement that tells your partner how far you want to go.

"I don't want to do more than kiss."

If you're kissing but someone goes beyond your limits, say so:

"No. I want to keep my clothes on."

If you are really attracted to him and hope to have the relationship grow, you could explain that to him openly:

"I hope you understand what I'm trying to say. I really like you a lot, and I hope we keep seeing each other. It's just that I don't want to get sexually involved that far until I know someone really well."

Remember, a reasonable person—while he might find those remarks frustrating—will see the sense in it. He doesn't have to like it, he doesn't even have to date you if instant sex is his requirement. But a reasonable person will not force someone who gives a clear "No" message.

2. *Stay out of isolated spots and do not drive with a stranger or even with a group that is "supposed" to meet additional people.* In the case histories of acquaintance rape, very often a group has "disappeared" by prearrangement prior to rape. With new dates, drive your car and meet the date somewhere. Insist on going to places that are public, such as out to dinner.

3. *Be definite when you refuse.* Speak firmly and look right at him. Research shows that the more definite the woman's response to his pushing, the more the man believes her.[55]

4. *Notice your fears.* If you're too afraid of displeasing your date, you may not speak assertively. A respectful partner will *not* treat you badly after you set limits. It is natural for a partner to be frustrated or disappointed—it is *not* natural for him to become angry and demeaning. Don't buy that myth.

5. *Stay sober.* Safety tests show that alcohol has a negative effect on people long before they think they are drunk. Numerous studies of rape indicate that up to *three-fourths* of all rapists *and* victims were using alcohol or other drugs at the time. If you lived in a society where sexual rights were taken for granted, you could feel secure no matter what your chemical condition. You could lie around intoxicated and your date would probably stop if you were able to say "No" emphatically. But since this is not the case in our society, you're taking a major risk if you use mood-altering chemicals with people of unknown character.

Acquaintances who rape often target a female who is drinking. They frequently plan to ply her with alcohol. Some researchers have found that *75 percent of their sample of college men admitted to using drugs or alcohol to get sex on a date.*[56] The idea, as one male student submitted anonymously in a class survey, is to "get a chick wasted and take her home." It's important to be drug-free to remain in control of your car, and also to remain in control of your body. It's becoming more and more acceptable to socialize without alcohol or other drugs. Sober people can still have fun and many consider it a challenge to learn to be at ease socially with no chemical props.

6. *Listen to your "vibes."* Trust your gut level feelings about this person. Repeatedly, acquaintance rape survivors say they had a strange feeling about the man, but did not pay any attention to it.

7. *If you're in a new environment, such as college or a foreign country, be especially cautious.* Members of the sorority/fraternity "little sisters" program on college campuses have had one of the highest victimization rates of any group.

Foreign media may portray American women as sexually available, and cause men to misinterpret your friendliness as seductiveness. After all, if *our films* are shown over there, it is easy to see where they could learn their distortions about Americans.

8. *If you have stopped seeing someone that you really don't like or about whom you don't feel good, don't let him into your place.* A surprising number of acquaintance rapes are committed by an ex-lover or an ex-boyfriend.

9. *Be alert to situations that can be misinterpreted.* For example, it might be practical just to sleep on his couch when you're too sleepy to drive home. But the potential rapist may not believe your "No sex" limits—and no one believed her date was a rapist until after it happened.

I especially lament the fact that women must take responsibility for avoiding victimization by someone else. The responsibility for the rape belongs only to the perpetrator. Once the Knesset in

Israel met to discuss the possibility of having a 10 P.M. curfew for women, since the rate of rape was increasing. Golda Meir, then the prime minister of Israel, is said to have replied, "The *women* come home early? They haven't raped anybody. Let the *men* come home by ten o'clock." But most men have not raped anybody either.

WHO HAS SUCCESSFULLY REPELLED ATTEMPTED RAPE?

Survivors of stranger and acquaintance rape report that their reaction to the impending assault was fear. Women who have *avoided* a rape *attempt* have also been studied, to find what successful techniques they may have used and what they felt at the time. Of course, they may have faced drastically different situations than actual rape victims. The use of force by an assailant is still the most important factor determining whether a rape attempt is successful.[57]

Reacting with suspicion and anger instead of fear seems to have made the difference for many of the women who avoided rape. But self-defense trainers complain that it is difficult to get women to act or even *feel* angry about an attack. Women have learned to "be nice" and simply don't think of fighting back. Imagine yourself yelling, "Get your hands off me!" to an intrusive acquaintance and check to see if you have a fear of coming on too strong.

There is no assertive technique that can definitely prevent all *stranger* rape. A person who would sexually assault an unknown person is not usually open to rational persuasion, though a few people have talked a stranger out of attacking them. This does not mean, however, that we know nothing about resisting a rape attempt by an acquaintance. Research with women who have successfully repelled an *acquaintance* rapist indicates that they screamed or ran away more often than did actual rape victims.[58] Talking back to resist a rapist also reduces the chances of rape in some cases.[59]

Rape avoiders also felt different *emotions* than did the rape victims. Women who immediately responded to the threat of rape with less fear and more composure were more likely to avoid rape. It could well be that the successful rapists were so intimidating that fear was unavoidable. But feeling strongly about your rights and knowing how to assert yourself can help you to avoid acquaintance rape in certain circumstances.

Another survey asked avoiders of both stranger and acquaintance rape what strategies they had used.[60] They reported that they used the following more than did the victims:

- physical and verbal resistance
- more forceful resistance
- more rudeness and hostility prior to attack
- screaming
- resisting immediately rather than waiting
- strong verbal aggression
- physical fighting
- running
- the most effective strategy: a combination of physical force and yelling

While we can learn something from this advice, we must be cautious. Women who are raped probably do not have the same options as the women who avoid rape. Studying how people act in traumatic situations is a very complex business. However, recognizing a threatening situation immediately and taking action has usually proved superior to nonresistance. Note also that an intoxicated person probably could not perform the actions that the rape avoiders accomplished.

Beware of Simple Advice

While screaming and yelling may help in many situations, a potential victim needs to think about her effect upon this particular attacker. Physical resistance has stopped some rape attempts, but law enforcement officials warn that oversimplified advice about avoiding rape can be unwise. Research about what *most* rapists do may not apply to *all* individuals.

It is asking a lot of a shocked and frightened person to consider her options calmly. But information can help you to be prepared. Only the potential survivor can decide whether to try one of the above options in these particular circumstances. Just reading this book, and evaluating your rape-avoidance strategies, will increase your odds of being safe.

HOW SOME MEN JUSTIFY RAPE

Three researchers asked college men what would justify their having intercourse against a woman's wishes.[61] The men rated rape as more justifiable if

- the woman asked the man out.
- the man paid for the date rather than splitting it.
- they went to his place.

Other informal questionnaires show that men may justify rape if

- she dressed "suggestively."
- she drank or did drugs.

It is appalling that any American man would agree to the concept of committing a felony over such minor cues. Yes, it is outrageous that someone would think you were consenting to sexual intercourse just because you asked him out or because he paid for a date. But over and over, studies indicate that *these confusions exist.* These are the distortions carried around in the heads of thousands of people in your society, and you'd better be aware of them. What women *intend* and what some men *think* they mean have been repeatedly shown to be quite different.

Making Your Intentions Clear

At the very least, women today need to make their sexual intentions clear when they're in any of the situations above. You might clarify your intentions as follows:

He: Want to go to my place? I was going to play that tape for you.

She: (Looks him straight in the eye) I'd like to hear the tape, but...we don't know each other very well. I'm not sure what you would think if I went to your apartment.

He: (Will probably say) I wouldn't think anything!

She: I like you a lot, but I'm not ready to get sexually involved right now. I just thought I'd better say that so we understand each other.

If he's a truthful person, his answer may reassure you. You've made *yourself* clear. If your date distorts reality the way some acquaintance rapists do, however, he may think you aren't serious.

What do you say if you're not sure what he expects when a man pays for your meals? Thousands of men take women out, enjoy the companionship, and still have clear ideas of everybody's sexual rights in the situation. But you may wonder if your date is one of those men. If you're not sure what he thinks, you could try to clarify:

She: You know, I feel uncomfortable when you keep paying my way. I appreciate your taking me out to such nice places. But I could pay my way sometimes, too, or treat you.

He: Why?

She: I know some people think...well, it's real important to me to be clear about how involved I want to get. I think, some guys expect something in return, they misunderstand what women mean when men pay their way. I like you a lot, and I want to be clear with you. (Here she may need to make a policy statement. See Chapter 4.) I need to know someone well before I decide anything about going to bed with him, do you understand? (She continues to make her policy clear and she checks with him on whether he understands. She waits until he *says* whether he understands.)

If he's truthful, he will tell you how he feels and you can make a judgment.

Suppose he really is a great guy and he is shocked that you'd suspect him. He says, "Come on, you surely don't think I'd do anything you did not want to do?" A reasonable man will understand if you explain, in your own words, why you feel you must bring up the subject:

> *She:* It's embarrassing to have to mention things like this, but I thought you'd understand. Some of my friends have had experiences where guys misunderstood.

WHAT MEN CAN DO TO PREVENT RAPE

Preventing rape is not really a female responsibility. What will *men* do to reverse this trend? Some men respect women and contribute nothing but their silence to our rape-prone climate. However, most men can become more sensitive to the factors that encourage a pro-rape atmosphere. Here are some things men can do:

1. Do not make comments that treat women like objects and do not brag about sex with them. If someone else does it, a mature and assertive man can disagree:

> "It's not that I'm not listening. I just don't like to hear you talk about her like that."

> "That's private, between you and her. I shouldn't be hearing about it."

2. Do not ply women with drinks to get them to do things they would not do otherwise. Express your disapproval when other men discuss this behavior:

> "You know, guys, I don't go for getting people drunk to get sex. I like my sex to be strictly voluntary."

3. Do not push women who say no. Speak up to women who seem to be giving you a double message and ask them which message they really mean:

"You don't sound like you mean it. I need to know what you really want to do."

4. Do not assume that you and your date want the same amount of sexual intimacy. Don't assume that her desire for affection means that she wants to have intercourse with you. She may want no sexual contact, or to stop with just kissing. Or, she may want some other kind of sexual contact other than intercourse on which you could mutually agree.

5. Let your partner know what you want through words, and don't make her guess:

"I'm not willing to have a relationship without going all the way." If you feel this way, say so. It may be a selfish viewpoint for a new date, but these words are legal.

Or: "I'd be willing to wait until the woman is ready, not saying I want to wait, but I would."

6. Remember that a woman might like you very much and still reject sex with you right now. She is just expressing her decision not to engage in a particular act at this time. If you push her, you may destroy her affection for you.

7. Remember that the state of intoxication of you or your partner is not a legal defense for the charge of rape. Rape is a felony. You can go to prison for doing the very thing that your culture is encouraging you to do: coming on strong and forcefully.

8. Learn to redefine a date in terms of a relationship: a date can be a success without sex. You'll decrease your chances of getting a disease, and even increase your chances of having a good relationship, if you get to know your date as a person.

9. Spread the word by talking to other men. Raping an acquaintance is not only wrong, it's risky for the rapist. DNA testing to prove the identity of a rapist offers hope of far more convictions in the future.

10. Some campuses and cities even have organizations of men whose purpose is to reduce violence against women. Give them your support.

11. Be a man of honor and tell the truth to a woman you date. College counselors report that, as sexual pressure in-

creases on a date, men may make promises of a loving relationship that they have no intention of keeping.

IF YOU'VE BEEN SEXUALLY ABUSED

Research suggests that people who were sexually abused or assaulted in childhood may be less likely to resist sexual assault than the nonabused.[62] If you were abused in childhood, this does not mean you are doomed to have other awful experiences—it means you need to take stock right now of your attitudes. You need to work on feeling *affronted and enraged* if anyone attempts to exploit you sexually. You need to remember that your past might have trained you *not* to get angry over intrusion and coercion—but now you will have to relearn. You also need to take your time before getting sexually involved, because you may have picked up wrong signals about doing what other people want instead of what you want. If you need counseling to understand how you can improve on these matters, check the Appendix.

TO AVOID ATTEMPTED STRANGER RAPE

It is not the purpose of this book to teach you about physical self-defense. However, there are precautions that will greatly decrease your chances of being raped by a stranger. Answer the checklist on pp. 237–239 in the Appendix and see whether you are up-to-date on measures that you need to build into your lifestyle.

FOR HELP IMMEDIATELY AFTER A RAPE

As much as the rape victim might want to shower or erase all traces of the assault, evidence could be lost in this manner.

Anyone who has been raped should seek medical help immediately afterwards. It's vital that you see the suggestions in the Appendix, p. 239. Many communities have access to a rape crisis hotline. Your telephone operator, hospital emergency room, or telephone book should list what is available. If you do not reach people with a supportive attitude, look elsewhere.

LEGAL OPTIONS

Rape is a criminal offense. People who have been raped can press criminal and/or civil charges against the person who raped them. Call a rape crisis hotline (See Appendix) for sources of help.

TREATMENT FOR MEN
WHO USE SEXUAL FORCE

See the Appendix for sources of treatment for people who rape or attempt rape. Referrals might also be obtained from rape crisis hotlines or some of the other resources listed in the Appendix.

IF YOU ARE A RAPE SURVIVOR

Rape is never in any way the fault of the victim. If rape has happened to you, you can recover from it. I know rape survivors who are now in loving relationships. Even if you did not use any of the above avoidance strategies, if you have been raped and have survived, the offense against you was not your fault. Each circumstance is different and none of us can predict what we would do in a given situation. It is human to react in a confused manner under extreme threat. Even the most well-adjusted people have had many experiences in which they've done something they regretted. I intend the above advice only to help you avoid any further victimization. *Never use it to second-guess what you should have done. You did the best you could at that time.* You are a survivor. Look to the future.

There's one thing that really bothers me about some rape survivors. They block out anything having to do with fear; this denial often results in their taking fewer precautions than a person who has never been raped! I've seen rape survivors go through dangerous areas without locking their car doors, or get into other situations even worse than the one where they were victimized. I know what is happening: they are so scared that they unconsciously block out any thought of precautions. The fear is so severe in these people that it has to be erased completely. *Please*, if you have survived rape, make a list of things you need to do, including those in the Appendix, and say them out loud to a dear friend or counselor. Tell the friend you're doing this to help prevent yourself from blocking out safety measures. Focus on how safe you're going to be and mention only positive outcomes. Ask your friend to repeat your precautions back, and promise that you'll keep them.

There is hope that we can all learn to respect each other's body boundaries and sexual privacy. Not only can you help to defend yourself with assertive techniques, but you can be an instrument of change to protect others.

CHAPTER EIGHT

Responding to Other Sexual Intrusion

For of course, when someone new
approaches us, we are all caution;
we take that person's measure.[63]

—Doris Lessing

The phone rings. Susan answers it.
"Hello."
"Hello, there. This is a friend of yours."
Her heart pounds.
Tentatively, she says, "Who is speaking?"
"It's Gary."
She realizes she's been holding her breath.
"Oh, Gary! You scared me."

You scared me. In our sexual jungle, the least uncertainty can become a threat. Hearing the unidentified voice of a man—*of half the human race*—can represent terrifying possibilities to an American woman answering her telephone.

PERSUADING, INTRUDING, AND COERCING

A person can try to get sexual pleasure from another person in a variety of ways—with or without consent, directly or indirectly, by force or peacefully. When John wants to be more sexual and Mary refuses, John has a number of choices. He can try to *persuade* Mary with words or nonforceful actions, such as touching her in an arousing way. If she isn't willing, he can stop trying and use some indirect and harmless way to get sexual satisfaction, such as fantasy or masturbation. John could attempt to *coerce* Mary by threats or by force. Or he could find another partner.

There is a great difference between *persuasion* and *coercion*. "Please," "C'mon," "Why not?" fall in the realm of persuasion, while "Put out or get out of the car!" falls in the area of coercion. Some people never even try to obtain direct sexual contact, by persuasion or any other means. Rather than asking for a date or approaching a sex partner directly, they seek unusual and indirect sexual outlets for gratification. Many sex offenders *intrude* upon your space without attempting to persuade or coerce you. Obscene phone callers break into your auditory space. An exhibitionist trespasses on your visual space. A voyeur or "Peeping Tom" invades your personal privacy.

You have a right to be free from sexual intrusion. Non-coercive *intrusion* is invasion of your physical surroundings or your psychological space without your consent. *Coercion* occurs when someone compels you to do something through strong force, such as threat of physical harm or physical power. "I'll slit your throat if you move" is such a threat; holding someone down so that she can't move is using physical power.

Sometimes people intrude unintentionally, as Rachel did one night last year when she entered the rest room at the movies. For about two seconds, she wondered about the strange little sinks that sat so low to the floor. When she realized she was in the men's room, she bolted out.

Had anyone been there, Rachel would have accidentally intruded upon his physical and psychological space, but there was no coercion involved. (Indeed, she was eager to leave the situation.) It is possible to intrude without coercing someone, but it is not possible to coerce someone sexually without intrusion.

How can we decide which kind of intrusion is more serious than another? One way might be to consider how *physically close* the intruder gets to the other person, setting the degrees of physical intrusion on a continuum.

DEGREES OF SEXUAL INTRUSION AND COERCION

The following list ranks sexual acts according to their physical intrusiveness:

0. There is no intrusion or coercion: partners consent to all sexual activities.

1. Intrusion is beginning, but the intruder's intentions are uncertain and he is physically distant: leering or ogling.

2. The intruder's actions are clearly sexual, and he enters the auditory or visual space of another: sexual gestures or sexual remarks without consent.

3. An anonymous intruder invades the other's auditory space: obscene phone calling.

4. The intruder further invades the other's physical or visual space with clear sexual intent: exhibitionism (exhibiting one's genitals without the other's consent) or voyeurism (watching another's private sexual experiences from a hidden vantage point).

5. The intruder physically coerces another person into contact with *nonsexual* body areas (such as a hand on the arm, an arm around the waist).

6. The intruder physically coerces another person into contact with *sexual* areas of that person's body but does not rape: touching of buttocks, breasts, or genitals without consent.

7. The intruder coerces another person into sexual penetration without using physical force: misuse of authority over the victim, strong verbal threats or pressures, or administering

a substance to the other for the purpose of preventing resistance. (In some states any or all of these acts constitute rape.)

8. The intruder physically coerces the other into oral, anal, or vaginal penetration, through sexual intercourse or by insertion of objects.

The legal definition of rape differs from state to state. Although the list classifies sexual acts in order of their *physical intrusiveness*, the level of seriousness to the victim also varies because of other factors. Most people would rather have somebody put an arm around their waist (5) than be subjected to the sight of a stranger's genitalia (4). The person committing the offense is also important. A woman may feel that a fourteen-year-old neighbor standing in her yard at night is less threatening than the stranger who cruises the alleys, looking for a lighted window.

All of the acts in 1–8 above are uninvited. They involve sex without consent. They do not involve verbal *persuasion*; they violate another person's sexual privacy. Although the experts do not agree totally on what constitutes healthy, normal sex, all agree that it occurs only between consenting adults. It involves no coercion.

Coercion of Men

It may seem at first glance that men are not victimized by any of the coercive acts in the above list. But nearly one in ten little boys suffers sexual abuse.[64] Exploitation of boys is a serious national concern. Males victimized in childhood often become sex offenders in adulthood. Mary Calderone, M.D., former executive director of the Sex Information and Education Council of the U.S., says we must educate now for sexual health if we are to stop the chain of sexual abuse. "Time is of the essence," she warns, "for the next generation of sexually violent criminals is already in the ranks."[65] Men can also suffer from sexual harassment. Men can even be subjected to rape. Those who are never personally victimized may suffer, even so, from the exploitation of others. Intrusion and coercion of a woman involves every man in our society. If a man accidentally entered a *women's* rest room, a woman who misinterpreted his presence could create an unpleasant episode with the police. Because of the terrifying sexual climate in this country, innocent men are vulnerable to accusations, and they should be as eager as women to correct this situation.

Would Assertiveness Help?

Because some intrusive and coercive acts are quite serious and harmful—either physically or to one's job or school success—no one can give you simple advice about precisely how to handle every case. You can be guided, however, by the fact that people who exploit others often count on their victims' compliance. They frequently fantasize about being turned on by a passive victim. Their power needs have been formed in a culture that links sexual conquest to domination. If you learn how to speak assertively to potential exploiters, you could reverse the "script" in the perpetrator's mind.

Just as bacteria cannot multiply without nourishment, sexual victimization can happen only where the climate is right. When a society subtly suggests that an attractive woman should be passive and an attractive man should be pushy and aggressive, this attitude reinforces the climate of sexual violence. If you don't think violence against women is a part of our everyday life, consider the fact that every thirteen seconds another American woman is beaten up by a man.

The Importance of Using Your Own Judgment

You can learn effective responses to various forms of sexual intrusion, which increase your repertoire in situations where you are able to react. But you should never apply advice automatically. You may need alternatives to consider, perhaps ideas for responding that never occurred to you, but nothing can replace your own evaluation of the circumstances. Do not ignore your judgment, even if you're scared. If someone says or does something sexually pressuring or seeks to intrude upon you, listen to your inner voice, your "vibes" and intuitive feelings. They are important. Then, if assertion seems appropriate, be prepared to say something.

UNINVITED SEXUAL STARING

A newspaper article in a midwestern city a few years ago described a male police decoy arresting another man in a public rest room. One of the charges was "making significant eye contact" with the policeman. And in the early eighties in the school where I was teaching, the new harassment policy mentioned "ogling" as a form of harassment.

It's risky to accuse another person of just looking at someone the wrong way. Few things are as open to misinterpretation. It's hard to define a facial expression. People who feel scared, wronged, and defensive may read all kinds of unintended motives into a look. Still, a look can be both frightening and intimidating. At a milder level, it can be annoying and distracting. If you think women are overly sensitive about how men look at them, at least try to be open to the possibility that looks can scare someone. While *you* might absolutely love it if someone stared at *you* with sexual interest, somebody else might find it ominous. There is so much confusion about sexual intentions that we need to consider where looking leaves off and ogling or leering begins.

It's impossible to make an absolute rule about what constitutes inappropriate "looking"; the boundaries keep shifting. Even in our country, staring is more accepted in some groups than others. What's all right in downtown Manhattan may not be acceptable in Salt Lake City. All of us need to learn early in life what is sexually proper so that we don't have to stop and think about what to do in every situation. In the absence of this early learning, I am going to try to offer some guidelines about what sexual staring, "ogling," or "leering" comprises.

Appreciative and Admiring Glances

If someone looks at you in a sexual manner, he may intend no offense. If you happen to have a gorgeous figure or build, even in your smart business suit you may receive occasional admiring or sexually interested glances. How long can a legitimate "look" last? In my opinion, if a person is looking at someone and the other person knows it, a look that lasts two or three seconds is probably not leering or ogling. Looking at someone for a longer time—if the person is aware of it—is called "staring," and if it is sexual, "leering" or "ogling." All three can be intimidating if unwelcome. People should be able to expect restraint and good manners, and when a person catches himself staring for more than a few seconds, he's supposed to gain control quickly and look elsewhere. It's also inappropriate to gawk at another person's body; in our culture, you're expected to look at the face of the person to whom you're speaking.

You could be looking at someone who has no idea you're looking. That is usually not considered an offense in a public place. If you have a terrific crush on someone and you're sitting behind her in a meeting, it's fun to feast your eyes. But if you were sitting directly facing her, it would become an affront.

What You Are Wearing

You may contribute to others' inclination to stare by deliberately emphasizing your sexual characteristics—for example, wearing a blouse that reveals much of your breasts, or a very short skirt. Men who wear very tight pants may also attract attention. Among heterosexuals, most people associate women with seductive clothes.

This comment from a woman could create an outrage in some camps. Am I blaming women for other people's behavior? No, I am saying that clothing can draw attention. You cannot expect to be ignored by those who are sexually attracted to your gender if you expose more of your body than is usually seen, especially in a sexually confused society. I've polled a number of very respectful men about this, and all of them think a "sexily dressed" woman is making a sexual statement. Whatever the female intends, there is research to show that men—even men who would never coerce a woman—may think the woman is asking for sex.

I especially worry about young teenagers who dress so seductively. They may think that the latest sexy fashion is great. But does everyone who notices them understand that, although they're making a fashion statement, they're not necessarily asking for sex? Those who wear seductive clothes may attract attention, but they still have the same sexual rights as those who do not.

Clothes do not give sexual consent; only words and clear actions can tell someone you're sexually available. In practical terms, howcvcr, when you're surrounded by people who are confused about your rights, and you don't want them to leer at you, you'd be smart to keep that in mind when you choose your clothes. They may leer anyway, but you are acting with greater awareness.

Outside of unintentional intrusion, some people stare at the breasts, buttocks, or genital area of another person inappropriately long or give the "bouncing eyebrow" kind of sexual leer. They seem to know what they are doing. This kind of staring from a stranger is usually more threatening, particularly to a woman in a rape-prone culture like ours. Men, not fearing sexual harm, may find a woman's leering complimentary or exciting. Or, if the man thinks the leering woman is bizarre, he may pass her off as a "kook," but he is usually not afraid. Being the object of leering can also be threatening if it's from a person who has power over you at work or school or from an acquaintance whom you do not trust.

Brain Wiring

It has escaped the notice of very few people that men seem to respond sexually to what they see. This applies both to heterosexual and to homosexual men. Looking at women's bodies, heterosexual men often show more interest than women as a group do when looking at men. Gay men also respond with excitement to the sight of other men's bodies. This tendency to be visually stimulated could be cultural, because of our teaching girls and women that looking isn't "nice" or discreet. The difference could be exaggerated by the porn industry. Or the tendency of males to be visually excited could owe partly to brain differences between men and women.

Research in the last few years reveals clear differences between male and female brains. Men often report sexual fantasies that include visual images of women's bodies; women more often fantasize about sexual feelings. This suggests that male brains may be "wired" to become aroused by sights. Our culture, no doubt, encourages males to look, but it may also have been an evolutionary advantage for men to be turned on by looking.

Voyeurs ("Peeping Toms") are invariably men. Very few women's magazines capitalize on nudity. Women can undeniably enjoy and become aroused by looking, but the emphasis is ordinarily stronger in men. Many men say that they find it very difficult *not* to look at a sexually exciting woman. I mention this tendency because we need to differentiate between sexual interest in what we see and staring to the point of intrusion. I'm acquainted with some very respectful heterosexual men, not one of whom ignores an attractive woman without some effort. Leering goes beyond this point. If you want to attract someone across a room, and you stare at that person, you wouldn't call it leering; you might even call it "flirting." Leering is unwelcome.

What to Say to Someone Who Leers

If you are the object of leering, should you say anything? Most people would advise you to leave well enough alone and ignore it, especially if the intruder is a stranger. Your remarks might be taken as a come-on or make you more conspicuous to him. He might finally give up leering at you if you refuse to respond.

But maybe someone stares at your buttocks, breasts, or pelvic area in such a way that you feel you must say something. A colleague may gape and ogle at you even at meetings where you become embarrassed and uncomfortable. No one can keep his professional dignity when someone distracts him in this way. You could make an I-statement to the person in private:

> "I don't know if you realize it, but you're staring at me. It's really distracting."

> Or: "I feel very uncomfortable when you keep staring at me. I want you to stop."

At that point, a considerate person stops looking. But there is no guarantee that a hard-core ogler will desist. He may not admit that it's happening, or he might even accuse you of oversensitivity. Again and again we see that people who are sexually intrusive hold distorted ideas about what they're doing and whether the victim likes it. Very rarely, an ogler may be so hostile that he enjoys making you uncomfortable.

If this leering happens at work or at school, it could be illegal sexual harassment. What to do about that is addressed in Chapter 6.

UNINVITED SEXUAL COMMENTS

What kinds of sexual comments are intrusive and which are complimentary? Many people are frustrated by having to squelch sincere compliments and affectionate remarks because someone might misinterpret them as inappropriate or sexist.

How a person interprets a compliment depends on the context. "My, don't you look lovely!" is not a sexual comment in itself, unless the nonverbal message from the person is sexual. If a person stares at your pelvic area while telling you that you look lovely, for example, that is sexual. It can also be improper to compliment a person's looks when she's engaged in some professional task. This happened to Brenda, a single mother who has worked hard to attain an executive position in her company.

Brenda's a bit nervous because today is her first presentation before the entire executive group. She is an attractive woman who has struggled to overcome sexist attitudes and feel like a competent professional. She prepared carefully for today's meeting. As she organizes her papers, just before she gets up to speak, Gene leans over with a wink and says, "Baby, you look fantastic!" Her heart sinks, and some of her old doubts about herself come back. She tries to shut out his grin as she rises to present herself at her professional best.

Such an uninvited sexual comment can be a jolt to a person who doesn't expect it. Yelling, "Look at the jugs on that broad!" is a sexual comment, an unwelcome joke about a woman's body. Experts note that intrusions like sexual yelling happen more often in violent societies. Though some women still encourage such remarks, recently people have begun to express anger toward them. Uninvited remarks about someone's sexual qualities are a form of sexual intrusion; everyone should have a right *not* to have his body commented upon without his consent.

A related indignity occurs with surprising frequency on college campuses. Pam describes the typical situation:

> I was walking across the triangle to my math class. As I
> approached one of the dormitories, I heard these voices
> yelling. "She's a five!" one of them said. "Hell, no! She's
> a two!" another guy hollered. I realized—they are rating
> my appearance! Some of the others were yelling too. I
> felt so humiliated that I stumbled and almost fell. Now I
> walk ten minutes out of my way to avoid that house.

Few people like being talked about as if they were mere
objects, even when the remarks seem complimentary. You can
yell about your admiration for a car, but a human being has feelings. Fortunately, a number of colleges and universities are
attempting to educate students about these actions.

Comments about their bodies may also offend men. A very
handsome man may tire of hearing what he views as irrelevant
remarks. He is probably not frightened by them, but when someone ignores what he is saying or doing and just looks at his body it
can frustrate or embarrass him.

Once in a while a female entertainer responds with a smile to
jokes about her enormous breasts. You might also find yourself
flattered when someone—even a stranger—whistles at you from a
construction site or a dormitory, or otherwise comments about
your looks. Unfortunately, however, your smiling acceptance of
these actions tends to convey the wrong impression. You're
implying that it is tolerable or even flattering to remark to a
stranger about the sexual aspects of her body.

This mixed message about intrusion being complimentary
even extends to violent actions. In St. Louis, a recent trial
involved two law students. In the bar where they met, the man
had bitten the woman, a stranger, on the buttock. She took him
to court. His comment was, "What's wrong with her? She doesn't
know how to take a compliment!" If he'd bitten her on the nose,
his act would have been perceived accurately as assault. Because
it was her buttock, in our society there may be just the slightest
doubt—was it complimentary? Won't boys be boys? Fortunately,
the judge did not think so.

What to Say to Uninvited Sexual Comments

There is obviously no hard-and-fast rule about when to respond to sexual remarks. The old wisdom of not speaking to intrusive strangers is still valid. If a stranger is inappropriate enough to comment on your body without your consent, this intruder might be more likely to intrude in other ways.

If you need a way to respond, though, you could make an I-statement:

> "Maybe you meant it as a compliment, but to me it is very intrusive when you comment about my body." (If this approach does not work, the offender may be so domineering and aggressive that he enjoys your discomfort.)

> "I'm hurt and embarrassed when you yell out numbers to rate the way I look."

> "I am getting really irritated with these remarks about my appearance."

You could escalate your assertion:

> "I'm fed up with having to listen to what you think about my body."

Or you may decide that sounds too "textbook" and just say, "Knock it off!" Such a sharp retort may work; some people won't respond to a civilized request and have to be treated with anger. But "Knock it off!" is not specific, and for this reason it may not teach the offender anything about the effect of the remark on *you*. Do not underestimate the power of revealing your emotional reaction. Letting others know that they are really causing you pain can be educational to *some* violators. Hard-core offenders may not care, but borderline offenders need to hear your reactions. Your negative experience contradicts what the "boys" are telling each other: that sex and scoring are all in good fun.

You could yell and holler and cuss at the people who make the remarks, too, but that kind of aggression might even encourage them. Some people would *like* it if they got a rise out of you. So you're already in a difficult situation. You have to try to figure out what would be most discouraging to this particular person. But remember, it is not your fault if you cannot solve this problem. It's the other person who is intruding upon *your* rights.

Harassing comments at school or work are often illegal, depending upon the circumstances. Check Chapter 6 and the Appendix for information.

OBSCENE PHONE CALLS

Scaring people through obscene telephone messages is against the law, but it is disturbingly common. For the last ten years I have informally polled my students to see who has received obscene calls. Through 1985, 95 percent of the women and 2 percent of the men in my classes had received at least one call. Since then the numbers have risen to 100 percent of the women in my classes, and approximately 5 percent of the men.

Unfortunately, there *is* very little research about obscene phone callers, whose intrusions have been regarded as rather trivial compared to other sex offenses. In a context that includes something extremely serious like rape, people tend to view other sex offenses as less important. But we need to respect the terror of a person who, in a society filled with sex crimes, is subjected to threatening voices in her own living or working space.

We pay little attention to *men* who receive obscene calls. When I ask how many men students have felt afraid or been intimidated by receiving obscene calls, very few raise their hands. There is a snickering, comical attitude in the classroom about these calls, which sometimes come from men and sometimes from women. Almost never does a man say the call scared him. When I ask the women how many were scared by the calls they received, almost everyone raises her hand.

Who is making these calls? Some offenders are young teenage pranksters. Others are adults with a compulsive need to make calls, usually while masturbating. A common kind of obscene phone call is made by an ex-boyfriend in retaliation for being rejected. Women in such a case should be extra cautious; ex-boyfriends also commit a high number of acquaintance rapes.

You can see the extent of some callers' dysfunction in the experience of a teacher friend of mine. Because she did not give her student the grade he wanted, he called her anonymously, made obscene remarks, and finally threatened to kill her. She had a tap placed on her phone, and when the tap located him he called her and pleaded: "Miss Jones, please don't prosecute me. My girlfriend is eight months pregnant and I'm afraid my stepfather will throw us out." Here is an immature, irresponsible kid living in a reconstituted family, about to become a father out of wedlock, and making death threats to a teacher who gives him a grade he deserves. He clearly has multiple problems. A caller who acts out a compulsion may be even more confused.

Responding to the Obscene Phone Caller

Should you assert yourself with the obscene caller? Here are some suggestions:

1. Strongly consider not responding at all to an obscene caller. By talking, you could legitimize the call and encourage it. This person does not deserve the courtesy of a conversation. He is an abuser who is violating you. Just hang up.

2. Consider carefully whether you want to say or do something punitive or painful, such as insulting the caller. Police often advise victims to blow a whistle in the caller's ear or to hang up. There are no surveys of obscene callers to find out what *they* find discouraging. I have some reservations about doing anything that might anger a sexual intruder. The caller may have your name and address. If you plan to take a more assertive stand than hanging up, you may be reassured to know that retaliation by an obscene caller is rare.

3. If a caller dials you again within a few minutes, you can take the phone off the hook. There's no reward in that beeping busy signal for the caller. You can also screen your calls with an answering device before picking up the phone. But an occasional intruder just fills up the recording with obscene messages.

4. Be aware of the common ploys used by callers. One is to impersonate someone taking a survey. This person gradually

asks more and more personal questions about your sanitary products, preference for nude magazines, or other sexual behavior. Another ploy is to make a preliminary call impersonating a policeman who is tracking an obscene caller. Police do not do this kind of work by phone. If you get one of these calls you should hang up, or you could say, "Police do not do this kind of inquiry by phone," and then hang up immediately.

5. Some women have spoken directly to the caller about the sexual issue. I suspect that if every obscene phone call were dealt with by this method, this offense would virtually disappear. But you would need to assess the risk involved. Rosa reports how she used this idea:

> *The last caller where I tried this was trying to get me to tell him what nude magazines I read. I had thought he was a legitimate surveyor and, being sympathetic, I stayed on the line to help him until I realized what he was doing. Then I said, "Look, we both know you're getting sexual gratification out of this. You need help. I suggest you call County Counseling. It's listed in your telephone book. He listened in total silence, and when I finished, he said, "Thank you very much, Ma'am." I hung up the phone.*

You might prepare for this response by looking up the name of a local sex addicts group (see Appendix) and writing it beside the phone. Or check the phone book for a United Way counseling group or other mental health center. Just think, all over America millions of obscene callers would get a referral for help instead of an opportunity to scare someone.

Again, only you can be responsible for evaluating whether to say anything to an obscene phone caller. It is remotely possible that a caller might be upset or even angry because of being referred to a mental health agency. Not knowing to whom you are speaking, you must use your best judgment along with these suggestions.

Although most callers are not likely to become violent, the obscene caller is already moving down the scale of intrusion and coercion that we saw at the beginning of this chapter. A repeated obscene phone caller is willing to get sexual gratification out of frightening another person anonymously, rather than from a real sexual partner. Such a person is confused and—while he may be too passive to take physical action—should be viewed seriously as a sexual intruder.

6. Your telephone company may be willing to put a tap on your line if you report frequent obscene calls. You need to keep a log recording the time of every call. Typically, the company then turns any information over to the police, who may use it in court to prosecute the caller.

7. Many women list their phone numbers under their last names and first initials to avoid identifying themselves as females. Some callers have caught on to this trick. In addition, of course, a temporary or permanent unlisted number is an option.

8. New telephone gadgetry promises to impede if not prevent obscene phone calls. Used experimentally in various parts of the country, these mechanisms discourage calls by revealing to the recipient the phone number where the call originated or allowing the subscriber to block reception from certain phone numbers. Civil libertarians are concerned because some callers might need privacy—for example, abused spouses who are afraid but must telephone their children's father. However, these problems could be solved by a telephone company code number which could appear on the recipient's device; the recipient, while unable to learn the identity of the caller, could report the code number to the phone company in case of abuse. This precaution would protect people with legitimate reasons for hiding a phone number. If every woman who has received an obscene phone call would pressure her phone company to make these devices available, we would see some fast progress in eliminating this kind of exploitation.

EXHIBITIONISTS AND VOYEURS

Flashers

Every city and every college campus has its exhibitionists. Exhibitionists expose their genitals to strangers without consent. "Flashing" is the most common cause of arrest of any sexual offense in the United States. In fact, exhibitionists seem to have a need to get caught, and often expose themselves in situations that involve the most risk of being apprehended.

We make a lot of jokes about male flashers. In one restaurant, I've seen a picture of a teddy bear in a raincoat, viewed from the back, holding the coat open and flashing. It's obviously intended to be cute and funny. The other art on the wall is pleasant and suitable. We laugh at flasher cartoons, because the humor catches us before we realize what we're doing. But victims of exhibitionists do not laugh.

In a country like ours where violent sex crimes happen often, women are frightened by seeing an exhibitionist. They can't be sure what he will do. Victims of flashers report a variety of emotions afterward, but some are so afraid that they even stop going out to their regular activities. Up to half of those who have seen an exhibitionist later report fears of going out alone.

There may be females with a tendency to exhibitionism. But unless they are psychotic and do something like running nude screaming through the streets, such women are not taken seriously. Our society encourages females to expose as much of their bodies as legally possible; and it encourages males to believe that seeing more of a woman is something to be desired—to be pushed for, in fact. These opposing messages cause many men to discount the seriousness of this crime to women.

Exhibitionists always try to surprise you, so it's difficult to be prepared to respond. Should you comment? One woman of my acquaintance suggests greeting the exhibitionist with the sardonic reply: "I've seen better at Woolworth's."

However, remember you are dealing with a sexual intruder. He is invading your sexual privacy, thereby demonstrating that he has some sexual confusion. Although exhibitionism usually develops in a passive man, occasionally a dangerous flasher emerges. It is probably best to make no comment to an exhibitionist until research tells us what such men perceive as a turn-off.

Your nonverbal behavior toward an exhibitionist may count, too. To the extent that you can disregard the behavior and leave the situation, you would seem to remove the reward. It may not matter if you show shock, however; Masters, Johnson, and Kolodny list only two cases where an exhibitionist hurt someone, and in each case he claimed it made him angry when the victim did not react sufficiently.[66]

Voyeurs

A voyeur is a person who gets sexual gratification from spying on people who are undressing, nude, or engaging in sexual activity. He may do this by looking through windows, heat vents, intricate mirror arrangements, or even cameras. Voyeurs often have trouble relating to women, and they sometimes commit more serious crimes. Rather than committing the offense in a public place like the exhibitionist, the voyeur enters your private physical *and* psychological space. He is a serious sexual intruder.

I've occasionally heard of women who attempted the "paradoxical intervention" technique when discovering a voyeur. One woman said she opened the door and loudly invited him in. I would not advise attempting to interact with a voyeur. If you discover a voyeur, your first job is to ensure your safety. Close your drapes; lock your doors and windows. Call the police. Then call a neighbor if possible. The odds are that you will be safe; *most* voyeurs do no physical harm.

Treatment for the Sexual Intruder

Voyeurism, compulsive obscene phone calling, and exhibitionism can be viewed as sexual addictions—compulsive sexual behaviors. But they result in a vicious cycle of embarrassment, fear, and self-hatred in the offender. There is treatment for these conditions. See the Appendix for places to find therapists or groups that help with sexual addiction.

Reporting the Sexual Intruder to the Police

These offenses are against the law. You should report voyeurs or exhibitionists immediately to your local police. The police generally treat victims with respect, but sometimes may not take these crimes as seriously as the victim deserves. Do not let that deter you.

There is clear experimental evidence that, after encountering an event that is *very* serious, individuals tend to react less to *moderately* serious occurrences. ("With all these rapes, lady, how bad can a little old flasher be?" "A phone call? Aw, those guys never hurt you. Go home and go to sleep.") Don't go along with that attitude. If you feel that a police officer's treatment of your complaint is demeaning or condescending, you can always make a complaint to that person's superior. If someone intrudes upon your sexual privacy, expect the police to take your report seriously. You are less a victim, you become a survivor, when you take action to help yourself cope. Get emotional support from others who agree with your perception. See the Appendix for support groups you could attend.

You cannot absolutely prevent sexual intruders from attempting to get their sexual gratification from you. But you can be alert, aware, and courageous enough to speak out against them when this is safe for *you*.

IV

HOW TO SPEAK UP FOR YOUR SOCIETY

CHAPTER NINE

Searching for the Causes

It is the basic taboos...
against "unthinkable" behavior...
that keep the social system in balance.[67]

—Margaret Mead

So far this book has shown you the necessity to talk back to sexual pressure and become sexually assertive for your personal safety. Now we will consider what you can say to protect your *society*.

But why are we in the position of having to be so alert and so on guard? What has happened that we find ourselves living in such threatening circumstances? What are the major causes, and can we control any of them?

There is no question that our sexual problems have complex origins. Many of the causes can be traced to family dysfunction, exploitive influences in the media, drugs, and shifting values. Most of these issues are complex and beyond the scope of this book. However, there are some reasons for our sexual problems that we have largely ignored and which our everyday behavior can influence.

WHATEVER HAPPENED TO MORAL OUTRAGE?

Moral outrage has become an old-fashioned, rigid idea. When millions of people watch vicious acts committed against their own kind, day after day, their senses become dulled. Americans have lost sight of what is out-of-bounds. And we calmly accept things now which once caused offense, including not only extreme violence, but also very subtle but inappropriate forms of exploitation.

Millions of viewers are captivated by watching perpetrators and their victims appear on television. Such shows explore topics like "Child molesters and the women who love them." Encouraged by a seemingly sincere host or hostess, the abuser and abused discuss their traumatic experience with all the emotion of a couple of friends getting over a little tiff. This courteous treatment gives the impression that sexual exploitation is not really serious; after all, aren't perpetrators and victims sitting there discussing their ordeal as total equals, as if all were forgiven? A simple confession seems to make everything okay.

Why are we not outraged that incest survivors are encouraged to sit and chat in public with their fathers about their violation in childhood? One rationale is the view that offenders deserve sympathy. They have often been victimized themselves, and they certainly deserve treatment. But some things, as Margaret Mead says in the quotation that heads this chapter, must be *unthinkable*. Otherwise people believe that they can act on even their most forbidden impulses.

Our culture has even brainwashed its own lawmakers. "But if you can't rape your wife, who can you rape?" This comment was made by a male California state senator to a group lobbying for a bill that would make it illegal for a man to force his wife to have sexual intercourse. Raping one's wife is still legal in some states. A female state representative in Missouri, defending her statement that some women ask to be raped, replied, "Gosh, you can't blame a guy—that's their chemical makeup."

Do the media—films, television, printed matter—contribute to these distorted views on rape?

The way our society represents sexual relationships in the media can be harmful. We have documented evidence of this fact. Because of the current depths to which our standards have sunk, the pressure for government censorship is increasing. Just censoring explicit sex in the media, however, does not get at the real problems.

CAN THE MEDIA CAUSE SEXUAL VIOLENCE?

A twelve-year-old boy in Rhode Island had seen a television program about a gang rape on a pool table. He forced a ten-year-old girl onto his pool table and sexually assaulted her while other children watched.

A few viewers, like that boy, copy some of the horrid acts that we use to entertain ourselves. But this direct harm is not our greatest worry. Only a few people who watch violence actually *imitate* it, although the results can indeed be disastrous. Those who worry about free speech argue that media research shows *no concrete damage to individuals*. People do not often copy the precise violence they have witnessed, and so in this simplistic view there is little harm from the media. Even more alarming than the occasional imitation of media violence, however, are the powerful *attitude* changes documented repeatedly by research. Those who look for precise imitation of violent actions may not realize that media aggression can contribute to society's acceptance of harmful acts in much more indirect ways.

Before looking at the research on how the media influence sex in our society, it is important to address the major controversy that surrounds the problem of changing the media.

THE DILEMMA OF CENSORSHIP

The First Amendment of our Bill of Rights says in part, "Congress shall make no law...abridging the freedom of speech, or of the press...." A few exceptions have been made to this principle: one illegal form of expression is speech that presents a clear and present danger, such as yelling "fire" in a crowded theater. Speech that incites other lawless actions and libelous speech are also regulated. "Obscenity"—which no one so far has been able to define—is also restricted.

Censorship is official suppression before publication or public display. But pickets, boycotts, and other forms of protest are not violations of the First Amendment; they are legal. Citizen pressure is not censorship. Even our own American revolutionaries, revered historical figures, protested and boycotted before they threw British tea into Boston Harbor. Without organized efforts to push for their civil rights, blacks and women might still be unable to vote in parts of the United States.

Our freedom of expression extends to media content that can hurt people. Some social scientists have begun to wonder whether the dangers of making another exception to the First Amendment are not outweighed by the threat in today's media. A number of professionals confess that they have been tempted to advocate regulation of harmful material after personally documenting its powerful influences. Some feminists consider pornography to be a violation of women's civil rights and have pressed for legislation to ban it.

However, censorship brings with it many other problems. For one thing, prohibition may not stop the abuses involved—look at what happened when we prohibited alcohol in the twenties. Prohibition began a crime wave, when otherwise honest people turned to racketeers for their alcohol supply. And outlawing the sexual images that people want to see does not ensure that they will form healthy attitudes toward sex.

Furthermore, if we censor, where do we draw the line in what is legal? Will some people want to outlaw pictures that help women find lumps in their breasts? Or discussions of condoms as a disease-preventive measure? And most important, the latest research on sexual violence in the media shows that some of the most damaging material would probably not be censored anyway. Researchers have generally found that watching R-rated films results in more acceptance of violent sex than witnessing X-rated films. Censorship is a very complicated issue. Far better is a fundamental change in public understanding of how media presentations can be harmful.

We need to raise the consciousness of our entire society toward the kinds of media that can cause sexual harm. Even if authorities did not censor entertainment that had been proved harmful, outraged citizens could bring about change. Our pressure on the media could change their definition of appropriate sexual relationships. There is such a thing as good taste and good judgment. Insulting blacks, Jews, or Hispanics is legal, but no longer acceptable in the media. Public disapproval is much more effective when people voluntarily decide to take action rather than invite heavy-handed government intervention.

THE FINDINGS OF GOVERNMENTAL COMMISSIONS

We have spent millions of tax dollars studying the effects of sex in the media. The 1970 Presidential Commission on Obscenity and Pornography found no reliable evidence that exposure to explicit sexual materials contributes significantly to delinquent or criminal sexual behavior. Much conflicting evidence came in at the same time, however, that documented harm from *television*. Among these data was the *Surgeon General's Report on Television Violence*, which concluded that people *could* learn to be violent from the mass media. Because of the results of this and a variety of other studies, many people were not satisfied with the Commission's report.

Sex in the media takes a variety of forms, not all of which do demonstrable harm. In 1970, not everyone understood that the government should extend its concern beyond the *sexual* content in the media. Critics of pornography, as well as its defenders, have generally held simplistic notions about the impact of sex in the media. But not everything has a single cause. ("What's wrong with this country is that other people don't go to my church.") There are not just two opposite answers to every question. ("Either outlaw sex in the media or do nothing about it.")

Not until the late seventies, when political groups became vocal about pornography, did more complex research begin on sex in the media. Because of the inadequacy of the 1970 report, a new Attorney General's Commission on Pornography was appointed in 1986. The new studies differed from the 1970 studies in several ways. One criticism had been that most of the early studies involved exposing a subject only *once* to the sexual materials; the new research exposed some subjects for several hours. For the first time, researchers looked at *attitudes* such as accepting rape myths, underreacting to sexual violence, and holding distorted opinions about jury verdicts. Researchers were now able to measure sexual arousal to violent material in the laboratory. In *For Adult Users Only*, Gubar and Hoff describe the difference in the conclusions of the 1970 Commission on Pornography and the one that met in 1986: "While 1970 findings suggested that no significant behavior changes...occurred as a result of sexually explicit materials, subsequent research was demonstrating effects on attitudes, perceptions, and behaviors...."[68] The idea that the viewers' *attitudes* can be hurt, even if they don't commit the acts they have seen depicted in the media, was new.

The Attorney General's Commission on Pornography concluded in 1986 that "substantial exposure to sexually violent materials is a causative factor in antisocial acts of sexual violence."[69] These findings echoed a number of other calls for changes in the media. Other government-funded studies by the National Institute of Mental Health and research from the American Medical Association have concluded that there is overwhelming evidence of television's ability to cause aggressive and violent behavior.[70] There can be little doubt of the need for change in how the media present sex and violence.

Before deciding what assertive actions would enhance our society's sexual health, we need to review the most recent research on how the media influence sexual attitudes and behavior. We shall look at these influences separately so as to isolate the effects of sex and violence.

WHAT ABOUT SEX WITHOUT VIOLENCE?

Erotic sex and aggressive sex are too often confused. They are not the same thing. Those who have tried to outlaw what is "obscene" have not even been able to agree on a definition. But "sexually aggressive" material is easier to define, since it involves more observable phenomena than does obscenity.

Earl, eighteen, reads a book called the *Kama Sutra*, an ancient East Indian sex manual with graphic verbal descriptions of nondegrading, consenting sex between adults. Are there any negative effects from reading this material?

Marty, thirty-one, finds himself powerfully attracted to magazines that depict sexual violence. Pictures of women being frightened by men turn him on. He loves to see a scene of rape portrayed as if the woman enjoyed it. Are there any negative effects from Marty's reading?

First we must understand the meaning psychologists give to the word *aggression*. It refers to behavior intended to harm someone or something. Earl's book does not involve hurting anyone. Marty's magazine glorifies aggression.

Aggressive actions, designed to hurt someone or something, begin at low levels such as yelling or being sarcastic. They progress to insulting, manipulating by lying, or dominating a person. As aggression intensifies, it involves physical actions, which we call *violence*, such as slapping, hitting, tying up, or bruising a human being. Some extreme types of media violence show a human being penetrated by objects or by animals, or the mutilation, torture, and murder of a human being. Such is the way we amuse ourselves by watching the pain and the wounding of our own kind.

When sex is combined with any kind of aggression, it produces a dangerous link. In the media, aggressive acts are often combined in the most intriguing ways with sex: a killer bursts in on a woman who is showering; an older man imposes sex upon a young woman who begins by saying no and then loves it; or maybe a couple are just insulting each other.

IS PURELY EROTIC SEX EVER HARMFUL?

Sex is a powerful drive, and most cultures portray sexual satisfaction and delight in visual arts or in literature. While you may be shocked to see private erotic acts, your personal response does not mean that they are all harmful; we must be clear on the difference between the merely erotic image and the degrading, aggressive, or violent.

Those who oppose aggressive sex in the media do not necessarily oppose all sexual content. It is certainly *possible* to make erotic films that are totally nonviolent, which depict a woman as an adult with her own preferences, not as an ever-willing nymphomaniac. Women Against Pornography, an action group opposed both to pornography and to censorship, contends that it is extremely difficult to find *portrayals of consenting, mutual, explicit sex between individuals in a caring relationship* in the United States. But even if we could find truly erotic, nondegrading sex where people were really *making love*, how would it affect children and teens?

A frequent diet of erotic sexual material may *ascribe an unrealistic importance to sex, or stimulate some young people into acts they are better off avoiding.* Suppose fifteen-year-old David and his friends watch one of his parents' explicit sexual films one afternoon when they're alone in the house. The next day David goes out with Nancy. They kiss and become very aroused. Mentally, David now has some concrete ideas of what they *could* be doing. Somehow it's more difficult to believe Nancy's protests. He finds that he's irritated with her. That videotape was so arousing that its images remain. In a way, David feels that Nancy is depriving him of what he should be enjoying.

Our young people believe "everyone is doing it." Sexual distractions can make it more difficult for them to concentrate on studies and social activities. Erotic or other adult sexual material may also *"sexualize" children before puberty, making them acutely aware of sexual matters.* Some teachers are noticing increased interest in sex at earlier ages. One middle-school teacher tells me that she frequently intercepts notes from eleven- or twelve-year-old girls. A common message is, "Would you let a boy f--- you?"

Our culture keeps sex in the forefront of everyone's mind. We now have pre-teens who dress in a sexually alluring manner, complete with makeup and tight clothes, becoming sexually active. We have twelve-year-olds who are pregnant or infected with STDs. When society implicitly promises that sex is the ticket to adulthood, imitation follows. On the other hand, some professionals think that, for adults, *erotica may be a harmless sexual outlet.* It may also be viewed as a positive influence. Sex therapists sometimes advise their clients to read erotic material to help them become aroused. In order to get truly nondegrading erotic video material in our country, however, some therapists must write their own.

Explicit erotic material should be restricted to adults. And that means *un*available to children. It is destructive and hypocritical to preach to young teenagers that they are too young to have sex and then intrigue and excite them by displaying sexual stimuli all around them. It is, at least, good manners to refrain from enticing someone with what he is struggling to avoid. And it clearly is foolhardy to depend upon parents to censor their children's viewing. Surveys indicate that a large percentage of young teenage boys have seen erotic videos and "slashers"—R-rated films that show extreme violence to women.

WHAT ABOUT AGGRESSION WITHOUT SEX?

One of my students says, "I can sit and eat while someone's head is being blown off." Our population is becoming callous and numb to injury and death. Police are beginning to report shootings by adolescents who talk about the incidents as if they had been engaging in a form of recreation. But even without sex, violence has an impact on women. Violent films with no sexual content cause more aggression against women than films that are explicitly *sexual with no violence.* That is, nonviolent films which contain a lot of sex may be less damaging than very violent films with no explicit sex.

Researchers at the University of Wisconsin found disturbing effects in men who had seen just "slasher" movies, films showing severe violence such as mutilation of women, but with no explicit sex. The male subjects were an above-average group, since severely disturbed men were excluded. After watching such films as *Texas Chainsaw Massacre* and *Toolbox Murders*, the men's emotional reactions to other filmed violence toward women was dulled. On the last day of the experiment, they rated the level of violence lower than on the first day, even though the slashers were arranged in a different order for different men. By the last day they considered the films much less degrading to women and less offensive than they had at the beginning. After seeing only three hours of the movies, the men viewed a rape trial they believed to be the real thing from a law school documentary. When asked how hurt the rape victim was, they underestimated the harm to her. They evaluated her as less worthy than did a group who had seen no violence beforehand. They judged the victim to be more responsible for her own sexual assault, and felt less sympathy for her on the final day of the viewings.[71] Other researchers have also found that men, especially, recommend a lower prison sentence for a rapist even three weeks after viewing common, nonviolent pornography (explicit sexual portrayals).[72] Even women in the experiment exhibited some of the same changes, but to a lesser degree than those of men.

Rape and fighting are both physical assaults. No society that encourages violence can keep its people sexually safe; the assaultive mentality knows no such boundaries. It is impossible to glorify violence to *entertain* people and separate this *nonsexual* assault from *sexual* assault. Remember Sanday's study of societies with no rape?[73] These societies do not glorify violence in any form, nor do they use it to entertain themselves.

We must confront the facts: *Showing male heroes successfully assaulting other people—whether in films, television, boxing, or football— is the primary form of entertainment in our country.* Female movie stars, who once had at least half of the feature film roles, now complain that they have less than a third.[74] The film industry aims at a target audience of males between sixteen and twenty-five, and this onslaught of macho violence has begun to overwhelm the public with vicious and brutal images and solutions.

Merely protecting the young from nudity and explicit sex acts in the media is too simple. If we try to get rid of only explicit, erotic sex, we ignore the R-rated violence which is the most risky even to adults. Violence against females is committed twice as often in R-rated as in X-rated videos.[75] Avoiding X ratings by substituting a new scale still does not tell the viewer what the film *contains*. The researchers report that in slasher films, men stab, rape, beat, torture, decapitate, scalp, cut with saws, burn, shoot with nail guns, or drill women with an electric drill, but if these films are not explicitly sexual, they are usually not X-rated.

Rarely does the American audience learn that most vital message for successful marriage, parenting, and friendship: conflicts can be resolved without hurting someone. Is it any wonder, then, that we see increases in violence at every juncture of our society? The message is, **when angry, hurt somebody.**

WHAT IF WE LEAVE IN THE SEX AND THE AGGRESSION?

I often ask my students to analyze the violence in television programs. One student wrote, "I did see a lot of violence when you gave me this assignment, but then I thought, if there were no violence, TV would be so *boring*!" Many young people believe there's no fun or adventure possible if we omit glorified aggression and exploitive sex. This tragically uneducated view, rather than reflecting the truth, reveals the limited environment of the younger generation.

Human experience comprises a wide variety of happy, sensuous, and frightening events. While violence is a part of some people's lives, it is the media's *overemphasis* on *irrelevant, unfeeling* violence used to excite an audience that seems to be the major problem today. There are plenty of possibilities for hilarious or exciting entertainment without glorified violence. And even great literature depicts incidents of sex and violence only briefly when it is vital to the plot. Hamlet had murderous thoughts, but his impulses were interesting to the audience because they were rare; people in Shakespeare's time did not sit around with an electric box tuned to nightly murders committed by powerful heroes and shown in graphic detail. And how many great pieces of literature or theater offer assaults drawn out in vivid technicolor, showing every knife against the breast and every frightened cry, to tantalize and excite the viewer as the woman tries vainly to escape? It is a recent phenomenon for an audience to see a human being inflict bloody injuries, rape, or death upon another person with such frequency and in such a manner. In the history of American film, there have been scores of fascinating storylines without this kind of emphasis.

The Humor-Aggression Connection

Do you think it has an effect when millions of Americans, *every evening*, watch people insulting each other as a primary form of entertainment? (If you don't think this is happening, check off the number of insults between men and women in situation "comedies.") On our TV, we actually have shows where dates insult one another; and married Americans reveal personal and derogatory information—all accompanied by uproarious laughter. Does this constant emphasis on aggression influence our children's views of sexual relationships? Of faithfulness, loyalty, and respect? I think so. There is documented evidence that children often imitate insults they hear in the media.

When hurting someone is portrayed as funny and a laugh track follows, it is virtually impossible for the emotional impact to hit the viewer. It is true that, historically, our entertainment has included aggressive acts, in Punch and Judy shows, the circus, and even cartoons where the cat smashes the mouse against the wall. But research shows that the more frequently we see aggression, the more realistic and human it is, and the more the aggressor wins, the more it tends to be accepted as natural and the more it is imitated.

One of the most common combinations on TV is sexual aggression with laugh tracks. In situation comedies women insult men's potency or intelligence, and men call women such names as "slut" and "bimbo." Casual, risky sex in a bar scene brings howls of laughter. Watching this type of behavior causes slight attitude shifts over time and allows us to accept things that we would previously have found shocking.

Listen to a randomly chosen episode of a situation comedy, "Married With Children," which has been rated among the ten most popular programs with Americans eighteen to twenty-five years old:

> The teenage sister wiggles her body—dressed in hooker clothes—as her younger brother informs her that the "Gutter Cats" are looking for a dancer. (Taped laughter)
>
> Sister: Oh, the Gutter Cats! If I could pick one group to have my baby by, it would be them! (Taped laughter)
>
> At the end we see the group has chained her to a fence; she is wiggling to the music and loving it. (Taped laughter)
>
> The father comes to "save" her (taped laughter) but he gets distracted by an offer to be in show business.
>
> Sister: Dad! Untie me! (Taped laughter)
>
> Dad: Shut up! (Taped laughter.)
>
> Sister: This is the second time this week someone has chained me to a fence! (Hilarious laughter)[76]

In twenty minutes this program enables the viewer to laugh at seductive clothes on a young teen, sexual promiscuity, unwed motherhood, group sex, male domination and bondage, the insensitivity of males who desert a female family member for their own selfish reasons, and a daughter with a self-concept so low that she allows herself to be chained to a fence not once, but twice. Yet the lines in this show were so cleverly written that the emotional significance of this exploitation passed by completely without most viewers' awareness. *It was funny.*

Desensitization

Research shows a fascinating tendency of humans to react less and less after repeated exposure to aggression or other shocking experiences. An incident in my own life bears out that conclusion. Attending a bullfight once in Madrid, I saw the big, beautiful animal, trapped in the bullring, look up with sudden shock and bewilderment at the moment when the matador stabbed him in the neck. As he fell dead, the crowd cheered. Even though I had known I was going to a bullfight, I was not prepared to see an animal killed for recreation. I was shocked to see these humans slowly trick an animal into coming close enough to kill it. I felt tears running down my cheeks.

Picadors brought the second bull into the ring. As they killed him, the spectacle brought tears to my eyes, but they did not run down my cheeks. By the time they killed the third bull, I was watching without crying, feeling more detached from the plight of the bull. I observed a number of tourists around me reacting the same way.

Now that much time has passed, I would probably again be sensitive to the killing of the bull. Since that day I have never seen an animal killed for human entertainment, so I am once again "sensitized." But we can view media aggression every day. One of my male students commented on his desensitization to a typical "adventure" program on television. In his analysis he wrote: "This program has shown rape, violence, and use of guns to kill people. I was not shocked in the least. None of it appalled me, and I had seen each act of violence before."

The increased tolerance for violence which the student and I felt resulted from the *desensitization* process. It is a normal human tendency to become desensitized. Perhaps this is even an adaptive ability that helped humans throughout history to bear traumatic experiences like slavery and plagues and watching their children die. Desensitization enables a surgeon to cut a human body, and a mortician to work with the dead. Research shows very clearly that watching television and seeing films desensitizes us to whatever commonly occurs in the programs. We come to accept without a twinge things which, if we saw them for the first time, would inspire anger, sadness, fear, or shock. People from nonviolent societies would flinch and feel their hearts pound if they watched the stabbings, shootings, and other murders we can see every day in our own living rooms. According to some estimates, the average American child between five and fifteen years of age has seen 13,400 people killed in the media by violent acts.[77] One year the ABC television network averaged twenty-four acts of violence per hour; NBC and CBS tied at seventeen acts per hour.[78]

The same desensitization results from repeated exposure to sexual exploitation in the media. We stop responding intensely to the near-rapes and insults, and the jokes and the teasing become a part of every American's commonplace experience. Where the word "bitch" was once shocking, even a rape attempt can now be received with composure.

Could the media contribute to this callous and insensitive attitude? Do *you* still have normal sensitivity to violence in the media? **Fright or revulsion after seeing media violence is a normal response. If you do not feel fright or revulsion, you have been desensitized. If you actually enjoy violence, you have experienced serious harmful effects, even if you are not aware of it.**

RATING YOUR FAVORITE FILMS AND PROGRAMS

How many destructive sexual messages occur in your favorite programs or films? On pp. 242–245 of the Appendix there are checklists to use while viewing your program. One checklist rates the destructive sexual messages and the other rates violent messages in general. It takes only a few minutes to evaluate the hidden messages in your program with this instrument. Test yourself for desensitization; if you are surprised at your total scores, you have been desensitized.

THE RISKIEST KINDS OF SEX

Extreme Aggression: Violent Sex

It seems logical to assume that watching a person who *does not like* being hurt will at least offer the sensitive viewer a chance to learn that a victim *really suffers*. But showing a victim who *likes* being victimized is the most dangerous kind of sexual depiction.

Once a few years ago I announced to my class, "Next week we will talk about rape." "Hooray!" yelled a young man in the front row, grinning and clapping his hands. Where did he learn to view rape as such great fun?

The National Coalition on Television Violence—which analyzes films and other media—reports that one out of eight

Hollywood films depicts a rape.[79] If you watch carefully you will find that some type of sex without consent—even if it's a comic character peeking in on a woman dressing—occurs with astonishing regularity in the movies. These intrusions are woven into the plot, and we may not realize we've seen them, so brainwashed are we. Recently fifty students in a large class had seen a new film. I asked how many of those people were aware that there was a rape attempt in the film. *Seventy percent of the students did not remember the attempted rape*, although a man threw a woman on the floor and tried to pull off her clothes. Her boyfriend saved her, nothing bad seemed to result, and so they forgot. Sexual violence is so common that we underreact to it, just as we take for granted the sight of a gun on the screen. Attempted rapes, violent gunfights, and physical assaults are a part of the background, sometimes not unique enough to notice.

Pornography—material that shows explicit sexual activity—is a medium that has been extensively studied by scientists. A surprising percentage of rape survivors claim that their attackers were either talking about or looking at pornographic material just before or during the assault. Rape survivors are not the only women who have felt the influence of pornography. Sociologist Diana Russell surveyed 930 women for the National Institute of Mental Health. A question was: "Have you ever been upset by anyone trying to get you to do what they'd seen in pornographic pictures, movies, or books?" Ten percent of the women answered that they had been upset by such an experience at least once.[80] Researcher W. L. Marshall cites three studies showing that as many as one-third of rapists and child molesters purposely use pornography either during or immediately after their crimes. It is difficult, according to Marshall, to resist the conclusion that pornography has a negative effect on these criminals.[81]

Pornographic magazines are not the only ones containing exploitive images. Aggressive or violent scenes are such a part of our culture that we may not even notice them unless they are extreme. Put a few clothes on the people, leave out the genitals, and you can get by with any violence without offending the American public. In August 1990, *Forbes* magazine depicted on its cover a woman chained down to a railroad track by two men, one of whom was raising a huge mallet over her head as she looked up in terror.[82] Yet *Forbes*, a magazine for the business community, is considered by many to be relatively old-fashioned and harmless.

A male student's response to a violent scene on a TV show demonstrates how subtle desensitization can be: "I did not find this violence offensive at all. I have seen that happen a thousand times. Although I find that I am more repulsed by the sight of mistreatment towards animals rather than a person. Why that is I'm not sure." Cruelty to animals still repels this student because he has not been witnessing its dramatization every night for years.

If we did to animals and children what we do to women in the media, there would be such a public outcry that it would be stopped in a week. The same holds true for disrespect to minority groups. No company would dare to sponsor a program that insulted minorities. But we've slowly been lulled into thinking that the scared woman and the violent man are a natural part of entertainment. In a sense, the media actually train viewers to sexually victimize human beings. They not only train viewers in how personally to victimize people, they prepare viewers to accept it calmly when *others* victimize people.

Rather than present the hundreds of research findings about sexual influence from the media, let's summarize the most prominent findings of recent, university-based research projects:[83] Most of these researchers use the word "pornography" to refer to the sexually explicit material that they study: Pornography can be nonviolent (mutual pleasure in lovemaking); degrading (there are insults or physical acts that are demeaning); or violent (somebody is physically hurt or forced during sexual acts).

The New Media Nymphomaniacs

A rapist was interviewed in prison. He had brutally beaten his victim during the rape. "She really liked it," he still maintains. It is quite common for a rapist to insist that his victim really enjoyed his attack—he may totally distort her reaction. There are documented cases of both stranger- and acquaintance-rapists who adamantly contend, sometimes even *during* the rape, "You love it."

Social scientists have studied this issue. Pornography showing sex between consenting adults, neither of whom is being dominated or harmed, is known as *erotica*. There are countless examples in art throughout history. An important modern twist, however, is in the *nonviolent erotica* that portrays women acting like nymphomaniacs. In these films, women are uncontrollably enthusiastic over any sexual suggestion or action from men: screaming for sex, acting ecstatic about any sexual request. Solid research suggests that watching a steady diet of this "nymphomaniac" type of sex, even though it is nonviolent, can be harmful.

Studies at the University of Evansville and Indiana University show that men who watched only one hour of "nympho" films every week for six weeks were more callous toward women. The authors reported that the men were much more accepting of such statements as, "A man should find them, feel them, f--- them, and forget them."[84] Remember, these explicit sexual films depict no aggression, but their woman characters are so turned on that they can hardly stand it and are begging for more. A number of studies have shown that "nymphomaniac" pornography causes many normal men to believe that women are more promiscuous than they really are, that women are always ready to be turned on. [85] Quite naturally curious about women and sex, inexperienced young males have few other sources of information about what sex with a woman is really like. They can't get the truth in the locker room and they look to the media. Pornography with the insatiable woman, our most common theme, is there to teach them false expectations.

What If the Sex Is Also Degrading?

Scientists have conducted research about nonviolent but *degrading* pornography. In this kind of porn, a man does something that may be considered demeaning, such as assuming a dominant position over a woman and masturbating into her face—and she is depicted as loving it. Or he dominates her as if she were a child under his control. In summarizing the results of forty-six separate studies by thirty-eight scientists, Zillmann and Bryant report some appalling results in both men and women from prolonged consumption of "common" pornography, that which is most commonly found in our society.[86] Although not violent, the sex is instant, it's between strangers, and the woman is invariably portrayed as a plaything who is eager to be used sexually by the male in any way. Look at the changes in both men and women after watching an average of six hours of common pornography:

Effects of Prolonged Viewing of Pornography on Normal Subjects

Sexual arousal.

Less and less feeling of revulsion.

Needing more and more unusual porn to become aroused.

Preferring porn that contains less common sexual acts.

Believing that unusual sex acts are more popular than they really are.

Becoming more tolerant of the idea of extramarital sex.

Viewing rape as a more trivial offense.

Becoming more tolerant of their partners' having sex with others.

Becoming much more tolerant of acts that are "improper" or in bad taste.

Expressing less desire to have children.

Expressing more doubts about the value of marriage.

Becoming less content with their partners' physical appearance.

Becoming less content with their partners' sexual behavior.

Believing child abuse is a less serious offense.

When male viewers in some studies had watched pornography that was even more violent than our "common" pornography, they became even *less* sensitive toward victims of sexual violence. Asked what kind of sexual force they felt capable of, many believed themselves more capable of forcing oral sex or other sexual acts short of rape on a reluctant female. And they believed themselves more capable of committing rape, particularly the more disturbed male subjects. They began to view violence as routine. When put into a situation where they believed they were witnessing a rape, they were less likely to help the victim than nonviewers of pornography. (Fortunately, all subjects were given a thorough explanation at the end of experiments to cancel any negative effects.)

What Happens If Aggression Is Added to the Degrading Pornography?

The most dangerous kind of sex in the media portrays women who *like aggression*—a very common theme in R-rated movies. The researchers describe this kind of pornography as more extreme than depicting a woman who is ecstatic over any sexual suggestion. It shows men insulting or even causing pain to women through beatings or other physical acts. They may be called names (often sexual: "bitch," "slut," "whore"), slapped, or held at the point of a knife or gun, but end up crazy about the guy. A number of soaps have also shown rape victims falling in love with the men who raped them.

These movies go much further than the women-love-all-sex films, which are not aggressive enough to be called "violent." The women in the I-love-*force* films are not always raped, but there is enough aggressive stuff to make it clear that *they like it rough*. And these films about women who enjoy or are aroused by violence change the attitudes of many men who watch them. In the studies, viewers became more callous and accepting of violence and they believed more of the "rape myths" such as those on pp. 139–140. When a laboratory experiment was set up where they could deliver a "punishment" of "electric shock" to a woman or a man, they punished only the woman, and they punished her much more than did men who had seen a purely erotic film.[87] (In reality, no electric shock was delivered.) Whether a male becomes aggressive after viewing pornography depends on a number of factors. But researchers at the University of California at Santa Barbara believe there is great risk to adolescent males who have access to this kind of media violence.

These studies were set up to see whether pornography can cause a person to become aggressive—to engage in harmful *actions*, not just experience attitude changes. Not every man in every study was willing to deliver more "shocks" after seeing sexual violence. Under certain conditions the subjects did not punish the female, and under others the pornography had a strong effect. But significant research done by the most respected researchers has found that viewers are often much more willing to aggress against a woman after consumption of erotic violence.

Is laboratory research really a reflection of life? Clearly it would be unethical to show violent films and then test how many people commit violence out in the real world. Ethically, it has to be studied in a protected setting. However, laboratory experiments on pornography are so carefully controlled that, if anything, they are thought to *under*estimate the effect of pornography on the subject's aggressive responses. Some studies even eliminated highly disturbed males from their groups and *still* found the viewers of violence more willing to hurt a woman. The advantage of a controlled laboratory experiment is that the causes of human behavior can be clearly demonstrated. The experiment is a powerful device for finding clear causes, which is why we respect the experimental method so much in medical research.

Perhaps you wonder about the ethics of exposing these subjects to seemingly harmful conditions. But remember, most of these subjects are college students, a population that already engages in a high rate of violence to women. Sexual violence is a serious issue on college campuses, and researchers are highly motivated to study this problem. In addition, the subjects are volunteers, and ethical guidelines require that they be informed of risk in any psychological experiment, and also debriefed (informed about the possible aftereffects and allowed to express their feelings) afterward. The evidence on debriefing indicates that subjects are even less susceptible to the influence of sexual aggression in media than men who have not participated in the experiments. The information increases their awareness.

If Pornography Damages Normal Men, What Are Its Effects on Rapists?

Only about one in 15,000 rapists is convicted. And one in twelve American males admits to acts that meet the legal definition of rape.[88] Since our experts estimate that 25 percent of American females are raped, we must conclude that thousands of rapists are free and unpunished in our society. They are often repeaters. The media provide many images that can appeal to rapists. When a woman is raped on a TV show, nudity is not shown. But even rape images that do not show nudity can have dangerous effects on rapists. Researchers have found that rapists become aroused by seeing images of a man being aggressive toward a woman, even if there is no sex in the images. This nonsexual aggression includes such behaviors as pushing, shoving, slapping, or insulting. Hurting a woman is a real turn-on to a rapist.

THE PROBLEM WITH MACHO MEN

What we define as "masculine" invites many of the sexual tragedies of our society. We should be deeply concerned that the "macho" male, the insensitive guy who loves violence, is much admired in this country. Some researchers at the University of Connecticut have proposed a "macho personality" with the following characteristics:[89]

- callous sex attitudes toward women
- celebration of male aggressiveness
- fascination with danger

Among psychotherapists, the idea is prevalent that we create an emotional vacuum in young men by squelching all emotions but anger. We instruct little boys not to cry, although it's a human, and not exclusively female, reaction. We somehow imply that tenderness is feminine. We encourage men to be constantly courageous and show no fear. All of these pressures can produce men *who cannot feel*. Those who score high on tests of "macho" attitudes show this lack of sensitivity. They express no interest in a raped woman's well-being; they see her as just an object on which to "score."[90]   If we socialize men to believe that the greatest achievements in life are power, domination, toughness, strength, aggressiveness, and the ability to compete, how can we expect them not to carry these values into the area of sex?   Millions of young Americans do not even know that "masculinity" can be defined any other way.   The primary feeling expressed by acquaintance rapists during the rape is *pride*.   Pride during a rape can be felt only by a man who values power and domination.

A young adolescent male is anxious to learn how to treat a woman.   He is more likely to see an attempted rape in our media than see a woman engage in consenting sex.   He is more likely to see her mutilated than to see her involved in mutual, erotic passion.   At one time, older adolescents indoctrinated younger males to the world of sex in the "bull session"; now the pornography and sexual violence that young teenagers consume is their "primary sexual indoctrination."[91]

I am beginning to form a theory about one reason macho men love violence.   I believe that, deprived of deep feelings of love, tenderness, and joy, they can allow themselves to *feel* intensely only when they are angry or watching violence.   When they begin to feel the more "tender" emotions, they experience anxiety, guilt, or embarrassment.   They become addicted to violence because it is their only way to *feel* without conflict—something that every human being needs to experience.

Females Who Encourage Macho Attitudes in Men

Is a sensitive man a turn-off?   There is plenty of reason to worry about young American males who receive their early lessons about sex from slashers.   But young females do not escape misconceptions.   One experiment showed that young women who watched slashers with men found the men *who did not react* to the violence more attractive than those who appeared distressed by all the blood and brutality.[92]   Has a "real man" come to mean "one who can watch victimization without feelings"?   Some women may subtly reward men for the very kinds of attitudes that could result in their own victimization.   An assertive woman does not usually find herself in this situation, nor is she usually chosen by a macho male.   Self-confidence in a woman is a threat and a turn-off to a macho male.

We have provided a superb training ground for sexual violence. If a Martian arrived on earth and asked for assistance in helping him learn calmly to degrade, torture, rape, or mutilate human beings, we would know exactly how to teach it. Our entertainment has made us experts.

FACING THE TRUTH

Sexual aggression in the media can change attitudes, change thoughts, and sometimes cause men to hurt women in the laboratory. These findings are based upon summaries of numerous careful research studies. The pornography researchers have gone to great pains to be objective. Despite many unexplored questions and occasions where research finds no effects, the major researchers in the field are sufficiently convinced of the harm of aggression in the media to devote their careers to exploring this problem. Scientists are engaged in additional research to examine further the complex connections between sex and violence.

Why do we ignore these findings? If many medical studies revealed, say, that a steady consumption of apples harmed large numbers of people, if the bulk of scientific studies showed that apple consumption created a health risk, apples would certainly bear warning labels at the very least. Only the apple growers' lobby would argue, "Not *everyone* is hurt by apples. Some people eat apples, and you can't prove it hurts them. Don't put warning labels on them!" When a drug is suspected of causing cancer in *rats*, let alone humans, it is usually withdrawn. Part of the problem is that, short of censorship, we have not known what to do. In so many ways, Americans sit helplessly and watch the social fabric of their country deteriorate.

Strong feelings have grown up about our rights to sexual material. There is an incredible ignorance of the research that I've cited. Some people try to portray moderate, concerned citizens as threats to freedom, and indeed it is a difficult matter to protect our rights to expression while protecting our rights to a sexually safe society. All of us who stand up on this issue must be prepared for criticism; but living in fear of sexual exploitation is *certainly* a threat to freedom. We have a *right* to go about our lives freely without the restrictions necessary to avoid sex offenders. We must have the courage to insist that we be heard. We must welcome the debate over this issue, no matter how heated it becomes. We must have a clear understanding of censorship issues. *Protesting the kinds of media that cause documented harm is very different from trying to censor art forms from which no harm has ever been demonstrated.* Trying to eliminate sex from all forms of artistic expression is an uninformed and oppressive action. But ignoring research about what is detrimental to our society is courting disaster.

WHEN IS IT OKAY TO PORTRAY SEX OR VIOLENCE?

If most young people saw steadfast examples of strong, caring relationships in their families, perhaps they could emerge from years of this media barrage without damage. But many of our young people face the onslaught of society's pressures with very little stability to which they can cling. Millions of young Americans have never seen a man and woman treat each other with caring and respect, much less lived with a married couple in harmony. We need to depict healthy relationships in exciting, adventurous stories more often in the media. We can make aggressive sex in the media shocking and in bad taste, just as we have done with racism. While some people will continue to hold unhealthy views, we can make it unfashionable and unprofitable to portray these views in the media. After all, smoking in certain public places is now taboo, but thirty years ago it was taken for granted. Attitude changes *are* possible.

Although there is some evidence that prolonged exposure to erotic sex might change what men expect of women, media sex between consenting adults is certainly healthier fare than exploitive or violent sex. We can even portray violence alone if it is not glorified and if it is realistic. If a story involves someone's being hurt—in war, rape, or even through milder aggression—*let the camera or the book show the real pain and hurt of that person.* The

National Coalition on Television Violence recommends certain realistic war films, because they do not glorify violence. In genuine sexual relationships, adult women dislike force and men reject force as a way of loving.

We must look for alternatives to censorship. If scientists continue to prove that our media portray sex in a manner constituting a clear and present danger, then further debate on censorship will no doubt occur. But we can take actions that are *alternatives* to censorship.

CHAPTER TEN

Becoming a Witness

Which side are you on?[93]

—Protest song by
Florence Reece
Harlan County, Kentucky

It is not enough to assert yourself just for your personal welfare. Even if you choose a purely self-centered viewpoint, you have a lot to gain if your fellow citizens are safe from sexual exploitation and abuse. Trying to ensure only your *own* safety in a sick society is like taking an antibiotic when an infection is rampant in your community; it may come back to you if it is not stamped out. You cannot remove yourself from the sexual tragedies of your society. You will pay for all the social services required to cope with these misfortunes. Your money will pay for police, health costs, therapists, prisons, and even for many of the children of teenage mothers. But most important, *you* will be trying to exist in a country where every fourth or fifth person is a survivor of sexual exploitation. Even if you are never victimized, you will discover that your friends, your spouse and children, and the people your children decide to befriend or marry may be among these exploited people, some of whom will still be suffering. The bell tolls for you.

This is a man's as well as a woman's issue. Men must begin to understand the indirect but powerful ways that sexual victimization touches their lives. Even one rape victimizes many people: the victim, other women who become even more afraid, and men who, although innocent, will begin to provoke mistrust and fear in women. In addition to the fact that men can become sexual victims, they suffer being the same gender as the identified perpetrator in nearly every sex crime against an adult. Men also suffer because they have been scripted to believe that it is masculine to accept any sexual offer without thought of disease or pregnancy.

It does not take a great deal of personal effort to cause social change. It just takes a lot of people who are fed up. We Americans have a great tradition of protest. Our country was founded on it. In a society with as many sexual difficulties as ours, those who want to reverse the current trends must commit themselves to standing up for what they believe.

"But," you object, "*I* don't contribute to any sexual exploitation." Your silence has an immense impact. To paraphrase Edmund Burke, "The only thing necessary for the triumph of evil is for good people to do nothing." *By your actions, you are a witness to your beliefs.* There is ample research to demonstrate that others interpret silence as *approval.* Speak up when you see or hear anything that encourages sexual confusion, degradation, exploitation, or violence. Learn ways to oppose events that are harming your culture. When average citizens understand how to assert themselves through protest, they can accomplish astonishing feats.

WHERE TO BEGIN

We need to put pressure on three points in our society:

1. Talk back directly to people around you about unhealthy sexual messages. Opportunities constantly arise to talk back in ordinary social situations: jokes among friends, sexist remarks in the workplace, sexual aggression in movies that you see with a date or with friends, and exploitive advertisements from someone who wants your business.

2. Influence the media to use their creative capacities in more prosocial—rather than antisocial—ways. Pressure them to educate their audience about possible effects of media aggression, and to stop providing a training ground for sexual confusion, degradation, and violence.

3. Insist on thorough sex and media education programs in all schools so that young people are prepared to cope with their sexuality and to understand how their culture is distorting their sexual attitudes.

We can make it socially embarrassing for people in the mainstream to continue accepting sexual exploitation. We can speak up to make sure that everyone knows where we stand; the clarity of our position will decrease the chances that anyone would dare to offend us by making light of our feelings. Such assertiveness is the reason why the media can no longer portray blacks as eye-rolling cowards or stupid servants. After years of hard work and protest, a social stigma results from presenting blacks in such a negative light. For the same reason, funny drunks no longer show up on television, *because millions of Americans disapprove*. You, too, can become a social activist. You can learn ways to make your society feel the stubborn ounces of your weight, so that we might tip the scale in favor of sexual justice.

HOW TO SPEAK UP IN SOCIAL AND BUSINESS SITUATIONS

All of us have been shocked speechless by other people's remarks, and have kicked ourselves later for failing to speak up. If we practice expressing a healthy viewpoint, we can be prepared for the next time.

When You Hear Degrading, Exploitive, or Violent Jokes

What you find humorous indicates to others where you draw the line in your values. But you can laugh at a joke before you even realize it contains an offense. Be aware when the skillful telling of a joke makes you laugh at something that really isn't funny. There are many jokes about exhibitionism or obscene phone callers, for example, that contribute to the cultural climate of sick sex.

Most of us have laughed at things we should have taken seriously. It is easy for the exploitive aspects of a story to go right past us.

One of my students heard the following joke:

"Why did God invent booze? So that fat girls could have a chance to get laid."

In two sentences this joke manages to degrade obese people, women, men, and religion; it also implies that it's acceptable to use someone sexually if only the man numbs himself with alcohol. And, of course, like so many statements in our society, it encourages the link between irresponsible sex and drugs. No doubt most jokes could be picked apart and found unfair to someone. But when they contribute to acceptance of sexual exploitation, we need to be more sensitive to the implications. In the last year I have heard a number of jokes about AIDS and even one about breast surgery. At a conference I heard a talk by a young college woman, infected with HIV by her boyfriend, who had injected steroids in high school. She confided that hearing AIDS jokes made it very difficult for her to be upbeat about her future.

If you begin to show respect for all human suffering, some folks may say that you have no sense of humor—especially if you are a woman. You might point out that no one expects other survivors to laugh at jokes about their pain. Do we expect blacks to laugh at jokes about slavery or lynchings, or Jews about the Holocaust? Then why should women—or anyone—laugh at jokes about sexual exploitation?

We're also stuck in the mode of "put-down" humor. But there are so many harmless funny things we have not even explored. And jokes can still be about sex. Learn to discriminate between an exploitive or degrading joke and a just-plain-funny joke.

You can make an I-statement in response to a joke, but if you feel uncomfortable coming on too strong, you could try to be conversational:

"Oh, I don't know, I dislike laughing about men's sexual failures."

"Well, jokes about women being pushed just turn me off."

"Why am I not laughing? I guess because jokes about _____ just don't seem funny to me."

"I realize people laugh about flashers, but I know some women who were really scared by one."

Suppose you do laugh and realize a moment later that it was an exploitive joke. You could always say,

> "You know, I laughed at that, but now that I think about it, that joke makes fun of hurting someone. I'm sorry I laughed."

If you want to escalate a bit, a blank stare goes a long way. Or:

> "I don't think that's funny."

> "I don't find that amusing."

For a more intense situation, or if you want to escalate your remarks:

> "I can't believe you said that. I know people who have been through _____."

Other kinds of I-statements can be appropriate:

> "I get so mad when I hear jokes like that. Don't you remember when I received all those obscene calls and how scared I was?"

Even to a casual acquaintance you could comment:

> "Could we talk about something else? I really feel uncomfortable laughing about this. Some of my friends have been _____."

When You See Movies or Programs with Others

Very recent research from the University of California shows that what women say, or don't say, about an exploitive movie can have a powerful effect on men.[94] The researchers arranged for females to view sexually aggressive films along with males. The study was designed to determine the effect of the females' comments upon the males' attitudes. In some cases the females were instructed to say that they disliked or were offended by the films. In other cases they were instructed to remain silent.

The exciting part of this research is that, when the females expressed their dislike of the violence, the males' attitudes toward the violence changed. The males were not as susceptible to rape myths or other attitude changes that previous research has shown to be a frequent result of viewing sexual aggression. But what happened if the female said nothing about the film's aggression against women? This study shows that a woman's silence does matter; when the woman did not comment, *the male assumed that she approved.*

But another dilemma made it difficult for women to comment: their fear of being powerful and assertive. Females typically express fear that males cannot handle their assertiveness and will reject them. The researchers studied the male's attitudes toward the female *after* she stated her opinions. The results show that the males could handle her assertiveness. The female's fear of being rejected was not borne out. This research offers perhaps the most important advice of any in this book, and it is simple: *tell him what you think about sexual violence.*

What a powerful piece of knowledge! Women—and sensitive men—have in their own voice the ability to change others' distorted attitudes. If all those who understand this issue express their disapproval, think what an impact they could have!

A woman who is watching a movie or program containing sexual aggression could make various comments about mild, moderate, or severe aggression:

"I don't like to watch that. The people spend so much time putting each other down."

"I know it was presented as a joke, but when they were all laughing about her body, I felt very uncomfortable."

"Some people may not notice, but I resent it when hurting a woman is a form of entertainment. I think it's sick."

"Have you ever noticed how they always put in something sexual where the woman says no but then she likes it? I hate to see that in a movie. Nobody likes to be treated that way."

"Did you notice the attempted rape in that movie? It's getting to be so common we hardly notice."

Or:

"I can't watch this. I don't like to see people being hurt this way. I'd like to leave."

Are you reluctant to speak up to people who watch movies or programs with you? Think about what that means. You have to walk on eggs and not defend your own healthy beliefs for fear of someone else's disapproval. Any guy who would reject you for speaking up about these things is already brainwashed. Your chances of a good relationship with such a man are very slim, if they exist at all. You may be surprised to find that many men are capable of sensitivity to sexual aggression—if only they have experiences that sensitize, rather than desensitize, them.

Other Chances to Respond

What should you say when a business or company displays something sexually degrading or exploitive? Suppose you see an offensive ad or picture on a product's packaging. There are assertive ways to convey your disapproval to the business involved. One young woman wrote a letter to a clothing company:

> I thought you might like to have some feedback about your advertising. It really turns me off to see a young woman in an extremely sexy pose, hitch-hiking on a deserted road wearing the clothes you're trying to sell. I won't buy from someone whose advertisements suggest trying to get sex from a pick-up.

We need to speak up when people make sexist remarks, and be consistent in our disapproval:

> "Come on, Jill, I really get irritated when you make men sound like they have no self-control."

How to Refer Someone for Help

When you hear someone who has sexual, drug, or other problems and doesn't know where to turn, be sharp enough to refer that individual for help. You don't have to be a professional to know where people can get help for alcohol, drug problems, or other kinds of personal problems (See Appendix). If the person has asked you for help, you could offer information:

> "I've heard of a place where you can find out about that. I'll look it up for you if you want me to."

What if the person seems desperate, but doesn't ask you for help? You could still bring up the subject:

> "You know something, John, I've heard you talk so many times about how much this upsets you. Did you know there's an agency that helps people with that kind of problem? I have the phone number if you want it."

SPEAKING UP TO THE MEDIA

The rest of this chapter will explain situations where you can have the greatest impact on the media to stop sexual exploitation. You may not be able to do everything you read about here. But there are some things you can do, and a number of them are very easy. If all of us protest, our collective voice can have a tremendous impact. Already, protest groups have persuaded the media to keep certain violent programs off the air.

Boycott All Products That Involve Sexual Exploitation

Do not buy *any* product that encourages unhealthy sexual attitudes. You may have to stop reading a magazine that you like. You may have to pass up an interesting cover. You don't have to pass up all sexual material, but in our country there are really very few scenes of "shared pleasure"—mutually consenting sex—depicted in films or on television. However, boycotting the products of companies who sponsor sexually inappropriate programming has proved a very successful strategy for change.

The National Coalition on Television Violence (NCTV) is a nonprofit, privately funded group that attempts to screen films, programs, and books, and pressure the media to eliminate glorified aggression and violence. They strongly oppose censorship, and publish a newsletter with their evaluations of the aggressive content of various media depictions.[95] While NCTV's job is not to focus only on *sexual* aggression, they do rate films according to their aggressive sexual content, particularly as it relates to children. Some of the films they recommend are highly entertaining. For example, they recommended *Born on the Fourth of July* because the violence portrays the realities of war: people *suffer* when violence happens to them.

Books may also influence your ideas, but the average American reads less than one book per year. There is a place, of course, for boycotting books. I refuse to buy books written by Watergate conspirators. (Why pay someone who betrays my country?) I'm not interested in buying books where people reveal secrets of their former lovers, either (that's sexual exploitation). But banning books is a dangerous practice, because who is to draw the line? People waste a lot of energy attacking books which they find personally offensive. These same people may sit laughing with their kids at comedy shows that portray men and women insulting each other. The book-banners do not realize where the major harm originates. Opposing books just because you don't like them is like favoring the withdrawal of a medicine whose taste you don't like. You have a perfect right not to buy it. But you need to separate *issues of personal taste* from *the findings of research* before you become alarmed about the media content that you consume.

There are also exploitive themes in many magazines; just look as you check out in the grocery store line. And what about public officials who give interviews to exploitive magazines, thereby boosting their sales? You can write to sensitize your public officials:

> "I don't know if you realize it, but the very same magazine to which you gave an interview often contains ads that are demeaning to a large portion of your electorate. By your cooperation you lend them credibility, legitimacy, and sales. I will not be able to vote for someone who..."

Black people have used this kind of pressure successfully for years. Every time you buy one of those issues, you convince the publishers that exploitive stories really sell magazines and make money.

Call or Write Letters to Complain or to Explain Your Boycott

Protesting a radio or television program is relatively easy. You can call the station and find out the name of the sponsor, producer, or program director. Letters are even more effective. You can note the commercials; if the advertiser's address is not available from the station, a reference librarian can often tell you where to write and protest. Explain what offends you and ask that the offensive show be removed. If it's unsuitable for children, ask that it be moved to a later hour. See Appendix for a sample letter.

Note the names of local advertisers. Call and politely explain your concerns. Sometimes sponsors allow an agency to place their commercials in the media without realizing that they're subsidizing glorified aggression. Most do not know which shows contain their ads and will be glad to hear your opinions. Be specific and restrict your protests to either aggression or explicit erotic material which is aired at inappropriate times for children. If you merely complain that people's sexual feelings are shocking, you may not be heard.

Thank Sponsors, Networks, or Publishers Who Present Entertainment That Contains No Sexual Exploitation

The publishing house of Simon and Schuster gave up a $300,000 advance to an author whose manuscript was found to be sexually violent. The publishers reputedly discovered that the book would portray a man who tortured and mutilated female victims and adorned his apartment with their body parts. Forty-eight hours after Simon and Schuster decided not to publish, Vintage Books announced their plans to take on the book. The editor of *Publishers Weekly* comments that Vintage has a right to publish it, and the readers have a right to read it. But, he says, "We also care that book publishing should not be so anxious to stay in touch with a perhaps debased popular taste that it abdicates its responsibilities."[96]

From such news stories as these, you can find media officials to whom you could write a letter of appreciation, or a publisher or network whose works you might boycott.

Picket Those Who Profit from Sexual Exploitation.

This action isn't for everyone. But make sure you are clear about the nature of picketing: it is a nonviolent and perfectly legitimate form of protest. Some people demonstrate for absurd or even evil reasons—such is our constitutional freedom to express our views. But picketing is a courageous and direct way to have an impact. Protesters have picketed porn shops, shops that rent slasher films, or theaters that pander to sexual violence. If you want to know more, the National Coalition on Television Violence will send information about strategies. See the Appendix for their address.

HOW TO PRESSURE OTHERS TO CHANGE THE MEDIA

Do not underestimate the power of a large number of people who demand labeling of media content. It may take time and effort, but it can be done. If you want to ask for a new rating system, or warnings, don't bother writing to the motion picture industry. They can use biased surveys to show that parents would rather have the current rating system than *nothing*, and they have billions to gain from the current competition for the most exploitive films.

Instead, you can do the following:

Press for New Labeling Systems for the Media

Consumers have a right to accurate labels; we cannot avoid sexual aggression until we know what we are purchasing. Allowing sexually exploitive material to enter your mind unaware is like eating an unlabeled food and discovering it contained questionable ingredients after you chewed and swallowed it. It may not hurt you, but you did not have a choice. You may never know that the aggressive image has influenced you. One method of decreasing the impact of sexual aggression in the media involves accurate labeling.

Consumers are beginning to demand that food products bear a list of precise contents, and no one considers that pressure to be harassment of the manufacturer. The freedom to falsify the content of a food product is not protected by the First Amendment. In fact, people get all riled up when they find an unsuspected ingredient in their food or drink: *how dare they* put something in our food or water without telling us? We should be equally upset if media content is not labeled just as accurately. We should be outraged when unlabeled sexual aggression has been foisted upon us.

I have found it personally very frustrating to pay so much for a movie ticket and discover that I have just subsidized sexual aggression. It's discouraging because I have always loved plays and movies. It's exciting to sit there in the dark and watch the drama unfold. But several years ago I began to realize that I was dashing out with enthusiasm to the movies and coming home not just disappointed, but troubled. Because of the subjects that I teach, and because of all the survivors who have told me of their pain, I could no longer shut out the exploitation in these films.

I remember when this insight first dawned on me. One summer many years ago I attended three films in two weeks. In the first, *Atlantic City*, Burt Lancaster played a character who peered into an apartment window while a woman inside washed her breasts. At first glance this seemed all right because the woman *knew* he was watching. (Remember that portraying a woman who likes intrusion is the most risky kind of sex in the media. The message is, women like to be the object of voyeurs.) Later that week I saw *Quest for Fire*. In this film, a primitive woman was raped by a man from another tribe whom she had vehemently disliked. But after the rape she followed him around lovingly and took him for her mate. The third film was *Victor Victoria*, a comedy. Because Julie Andrews' uncertain gender was part of the plot, James Garner hid in a closet to peek at her. Somehow it didn't really seem like something sexual happened without consent.

There's room for an occasional comedy like *Victor Victoria*. There's a place for an infrequent drama about rape. But for me it was a shock to realize that *in my country it is hard to find entertainment without the little moment of sexual nonconsent.*

In the years before and since, we have had major films with nonconsensual sex. It was not always a rape—sometimes just a hint of sexual force was enough to satisfy the moviemakers that they could make money off of us. In *Psycho*, a beautiful woman in a shower is stabbed by a crazed madman. In *Stakeout*, the hero who eventually got the girl hid under her bed and watched her undress. *The Deep* portrayed one of the bad guys drawing a knife down the very sexy belly of Jacqueline Bisset; would he rape her? We weren't sure. *Pretty Woman*, a big hit, contained a rather prolonged attempted rape. *Ghost*, in the same year, portrayed a crazed madman who stumbled upon the female lead and began to watch her undress, licking his lips, but her cat scared him off. Even *White Palace* had an instance of nonconsensual sex, and almost no one noticed: a young widower, intoxicated, was too drunk to drive home and slept at the house of an older woman who was trying to seduce him. He was still grieving over his wife, and he refused. She implied that she would allow him to sleep it off on her couch, but in the middle of the night she began to arouse him as he slept and her seduction began a mad, passionate affair. To have sex with someone who is intoxicated and has refused consent qualifies as *rape* in some states. But since the character liked it, the film imparts the belief that *saying no is meaningless*.

The numerous acts of nonconsensual sex in American films range from subtle to blatant, and filmmakers make billions from sexual exploitation. We are being manipulated on a massive scale. *Only we* can teach filmmakers different attitudes. And *only labels* can tell us what is in the film before we watch it. Had I known about the content of any of those films, I would not have attended. Not because I don't want to be entertained, not because there was sex in the films, but because I think boycotting is our chief way to send a resounding message to the entertainment industry: *We are noticing the nonconsenting sex you are foisting upon us, and we won't buy it.* I was entertained by parts of those films. But I would rather give up the enjoyment of those few scenes than financially support the filmmakers who use sexual force for profit.

Unlike the public acceptance of our inadequate film ratings, an immense controversy has developed about labeling the sexual content of records. 2 Live Crew, for example, has recorded a song about a man sexually abusing a woman until she "walks funny." The song says he will "break her backbone" and "bust her p----."[97]

This verbal aggression suggests why some Americans who value the Bill of Rights still favor accurate labels and warnings.

NCTV News reports that major songwriters' and publishers' associations have declined or hesitated to oppose the proposed labeling laws, "a clear sign that even people in the recording industry believe things have gone too far."[98]

Our film rating system is not labeling. It is totally inadequate, for rather than labeling the "ingredients" of the film, the industry decides how appropriate the film is, and they rate it (X, R, G, etc.) for us. They rate it, not according to what is in it, but as a parent would, according to *who can see it*. There exists no real labeling system for television; and you can find yourself watching sexual put-downs, dishonesty, or exploitation under such deceptively innocent titles that you expected to see a warm family show. The absence of labels makes it impossible for anyone to evaluate what is suitable, although a number of professional groups have reached conclusions like those of the American Academy of Pediatrics: "Protracted television viewing is one cause of violent or aggressive behavior."[99] We have a *right* to know what we're going to be seeing and hearing. We can improve our labeling system and still keep the restrictions against children seeing harmful material; such actions are fully compatible with the First Amendment.

The National Coalition on Television Violence has recommended the following movie rating system:[100]

PG—some non-harmful material that requires some adult guidance for children to understand correctly.

PGV—this violence may frighten some young children, but probably does not teach violence.

R13—this violence probably has some harmful effect, promoting minor amounts of violence, antisocial themes that parents should discourage, or the film may contain mature sexual material that may not be suitable for children to view.

RM—this kind of movie is not considered harmful, but viewing it shows material, especially nondegrading sexual material of a loving and caring nature, that should be restricted to a mature, adult viewing audience.

R18—films contain sexual material of a harmful nature (or harmful material other than violence, such as drug use), with more than minor harmful antisocial effects.

RV—films are likely to cause viewers to become prone to anger and violence according to existing research studies, but the violence is not especially gruesome, sadistic, graphic, or intense.

X—films with serious exploitive or degrading sexual content as the main effect.

XV—for high levels of intense violence of a very harmful nature, where violence is strongly glamorized or used to excite.

X-Unfit—extreme or sadistic violence with graphic or gruesome characteristics. Intensely callous and degrading sexual material, especially when associated with violence, tends to fall into this category.

This rating system is based on the idea that ratings should inform people. Their *ratings* are partially *labels*—that is, they inform the public about the content of films. This system would let the viewer know which films were merely erotic, which contained violence that research has found harmful, which were nonviolent but harmful, exploitive or degrading sexually, or "unfit."

NCTV monitors acts of violence in several media; the resulting "scores" include counts of the actual acts of violence per hour in a given movie. The scores give a greater weight to depictions of murder or rape. We might need to enlist the help of our top researchers to clarify and refine this system even further.

Ask for Prebriefings and Debriefings

Researchers have provided us with some powerful new guidelines to reduce the harm violent media may otherwise cause. One unique way to decrease the effects of exploitive sex is simply to tell the viewer specifically about its harmful effects. Each film or TV piece would include some kind of "prebriefing" and "debriefing" at the beginning and end. This information would be more than the kind of warnings that cigarettes and alcohol contain, brief cautions which one can easily ignore. The briefing explains as precisely as possible what the negative effects may be, and they correct myths and other misinformation implied by the film.

Research on sexual aggression shows that people who view it are essentially unaware of its slow but subtle effect on their attitudes. Discussion, however, or listening to a statement about possible harm from a film, can cause attitudes to remain healthier and more rational.[101]   A number of studies found that properly debriefed viewers of a violent rape do not form the callous view that rape is trivial and common.[102]   This effect also explains why researchers, who have insight into media influence, do not suffer harm from their work.   They are continually being "debriefed," so that they understand the manipulations of media presentations. *Awareness sensitizes the viewer.*

A prebriefing to precede an exploitive film could be the following:

> *What you are about to see depicts people sexually exploiting each other. Research indicates that people who see degrading, insulting, or violent sex may gradually stop feeling shock or disapproval. In addition, other damaging attitude changes can occur in people who view sexually exploitive films. This film also depicts women as willing and eager to participate in any sexual act that a man wants. This view is not accurate. Normal women may like or dislike particular sex acts, and do not always respond enthusiastically to the sexual suggestions of a partner.*

This would be similar to legally required explanations in flyers that accompany medicines.   But because a briefing *explains* as well as warns, it is quite different from alcohol and cigarette warnings. Such a *de*briefing could also follow a program or film:

> *What you have just seen depicts a woman enjoying a rape. This is not an accurate view. Rape is a serious crime which often causes serious psychological problems in the victim. Rapists can be punished by many years in prison. A common but false belief is that women secretly desire to be raped, or enjoy sexual force. This film also implies that rape is normal for men. Neither of these assumptions is true. Rape is an abnormal act committed more from anger and power than sexual motives. Research shows that watching violent pornography like this may cause viewers to think that sexual violence is less serious than it really is.*

Pre- and debriefings will not work if they are a mere canned "caution" put on all products.   They need to be specifically written to neutralize the distorted messages being sent by a particular portrayal.   Experts who do the research on this educational technique could help us design appropriate briefings for films, television material, and even books and magazines. Three of our foremost media researchers recommend that "public service announcements should precede and/or follow television programs that even hint at the justification of violence against women."[103]

You say, this will never work? Why not? We now have warnings on cigarettes and alcohol. And, while they might scare off a few people, those mere "warnings" have far less chance of helping by far than *briefings* of media violence. There is no proof that warnings on cigarettes and alcohol actually lessen their harmful effects, but there *is* evidence that prebriefings and debriefings can decrease the damage of exploitive sex in the media. If we knew of a warning that decreased or completely eliminated the health risks of cigarettes and alcohol, do you think we should require that it be included on the product? That's how promising prebriefings and debriefings are. And just as medical labels come from medical experts, media labels should be written by experts on aggression in the media. Our goal is to sweep through our entire society with information like the campaigns to inform Americans about the effects of cholesterol or air pollution.

Briefings would not make pornographic material acceptable for children, of course. Regardless of labels or explanations of harm, children should still be protected from watching sexual exploitation of any kind.

WHERE TO ASK FOR THESE CHANGES

If you're determined to influence the portrayal of sex in the media, be prepared to meet people who might seem appallingly different from you. Although you may have learned from the research presented here that *aggression* is the major issue, others may view *explicit sex* as the culprit. It is unquestionably a bit of a strain to join ranks with someone who is miles away from you philosophically. But can we afford to be that choosy? If we can find people with the same general goals—drastically reducing sexual exploitation in the media without censorship—we will need to align with them.

If a political conservative hates rape films for one reason and a civil libertarian for other reasons, perhaps they can find a common ground. Most successful political alliances in this country have been made by people willing to ignore differences that are irrelevant to their goals.

Write your legislators: your state senators and representatives, and your U.S. senators and representatives in Congress. If you need to know their names and addresses, call the League of Women Voters in your area. Ask for accurate labeling and explain prebriefings and debriefings. Explain any intentions you may have to vote against politicians who support sexual exploitation by, for example, giving interviews to magazines that make money from exploitive articles, ads, or pictures.

Join local groups that are active in demanding labeling and rating changes. The Junior League has been very effective in this battle. If there is a Junior League in your area, call and find out what you can do. Recruit people to help from churches and temples, PTAs, and other community groups. Be prepared to pursue the subject through a number of phone calls.

Form a local labeling board. Some cities have a public rating board that rates films for use in local theaters. The Supreme Court has found that it is constitutional for a community to rate the films shown there. If you can use a *labeling* system, similar to that on pp. 220–221, consumers will find themselves able to make even more safe and intelligent choices.

Write or call the Federal Communications Commission to complain or suggest or urge that the FCC require high-quality children's programming of an educational and instructional nature as a condition of license renewal for television stations. See the Appendix for the address of the FCC.

Join or contribute to national organizations that agree with your views. Put your money where your mouth is. Choose carefully from your own contacts or from the organizations listed in the Appendix.

SPEAKING UP FOR CHILDREN

There is no question that childhood influences can stay with us for life. Children can learn permanent attitudes at birth; I have even known several people born with the umbilical cord around their necks who as adults could not bear to wear turtlenecks or mufflers, but had never made the connection. The immature brain has an awesome ability to latch on to experiences and learn permanent attitudes or emotions from childhood events. Most of our struggles with ourselves involve "getting past the past." Childhood is the foundation on which the adult personality is formed, and invariably therapists find that sex offenders suffer from early influences.

But children don't just absorb unhealthy attitudes from the family. The more sick a *society*, the more distorted attitudes form in the average child. If we care about our society, we will do all we can to protect its children. In a real sense, *they are ours*.

How to Report Child Abuse

Abusing a child physically or sexually is one of the principal ways to set a human being on the path of victimizing others. Although some survivors escape without ever abusing others, most sex offenders have been abused either sexually or physically. It's hard to believe that an innocent little child could grow up to hurt other people. But it happens frequently.

Suspecting child abuse automatically creates a responsibility. *You may be the only person in the world who suspects that this child is being abused and who can defend him.* Don't buy into the fear of being a "tattletale"—that is just a hangover from elementary school. Don't let him down; if you even *suspect* any form of abuse, call your state's Child Abuse Hotline. If you're concerned about anonymity or other procedures, check by calling the hotline first and asking about these matters. (See Appendix.)

Supervising Television

It is naive to assume that most parents supervise television; TV is an excellent babysitter and has all the elements that command human attention: movement, sound, and contrast. Parents who enforce television rules need time, energy, and an absence of distractions. Even then, thousands of parents are not well informed about media harm or focused enough to put supervision high in their priorities. The most dysfunctional families—whose children are most susceptible to media influence—are the *least* likely families to supervise TV.

Some parents don't even care if their kids are on drugs, much less whether they are being sexualized. Many others care, but are too preoccupied with problems. And what kind of sense does it make to put a powerfully attractive box in one's living room filled with tantalizing, harmful pictures, and then tell children not to watch? If drug companies sold delicious, eye-catching medicines in bottles with no safety lids, we would be up in arms. We should be equally concerned about attractive but potentially harmful media presentations that our children can watch with no constraints. It is possible to film exciting, adventurous stories where passion and anger are present, yet exploitive sex and glorified violence are absent. The media must become responsible for what they offer to the public. Unfortunately, most media and their sponsors will take up that responsibility only if they learn that it sells more tickets and products than does exploitation.

Whenever you view any form of exploitive or aggressive sex in the presence of a child, you have a chance to do your own editorializing. The child would preferably not watch harmful programs. But if something damaging comes on television unexpectedly, you can interrupt the kids' program:

> "I don't like to hear people laugh and call each other bad names. Sometimes we get mad at each other, but we don't call each other bad names."

Or, if you're speaking to a teenager,

> "I really get upset over this program. What do you think would happen if people really treated each other like

this? They make it look like people can't solve any problems without hurting someone. What do you think?"

You can editorialize (debrief) about pornography as well. Norma Ramos, the general counsel for Women Against Pornography, says that parents must become aware of how to influence children not to participate in this epidemic of sexual exploitation. "We have to stop socializing boys the way we do," she says. "When parents see their sons reading pornography, they should engage them in a *real* serious dialogue. What are the messages that are being sent to your son?"[104]

I suggest that if you find your little brother or your child reading any sexually degrading material, even if it is "nonviolent" and merely makes women look like idiot playthings, you comment:

> "I notice you're reading _____. What do you think about that?"
>
> He'll probably say: "Nothin'."
>
> You could say: "You know why I don't like to see you looking at this stuff? Because people aren't really like these people, this isn't what people do. This magazine makes women look_____, and men _____."

You can elaborate according to your views. Remember, you're not just whistling in the wind. There is solid research to indicate that when you make remarks about how unrealistic and unhealthy a program is, you can change attitudes in adults or children. You are *debriefing!* I hope you don't let any opportunities pass. Research evidence also indicates that when there is no adult commenting to the contrary, children tend to think what they're doing is okay.

Insist on Adequate Sex Education

One reason parents are scared about sex education is that they don't know what values the teachers are going to impart to their children. There are some issues, such as abortion, that are so controversial no program containing the subject would ever pass the current political climate. Why not leave out abortion and agree on the *basics* of health education? In addition to the biological facts, *all* children should learn the skills of resisting sexual pressure—how to avoid molestation in the early years and use sexual assertiveness in all the years following. *All* children, even before they are old enough to get into sexual trouble, should learn about disease and pregnancy prevention as well as the reasons why they are too young for sex. And yet, the skillful teacher can still avoid making sex sound like a scary thing; the approach should stress planning and responsibility.

If some teachers don't know how to do that, we must find the funds for more teacher training. Excellent teachers can put sexual safety in a wise and cautious context. Parents often fear that, by discussing sex openly and honestly, teachers will encourage sexual activity. The research does not bear out this fear. A skilled teacher can avoid *endorsing* premarital sex, but can teach about disease and pregnancy as subjects students will need to know at some point in their lives. We do, after all, teach about many things that students may not immediately use.

Encouraging studies show that we can prevent the media from damaging our children through *specific educational techniques*. Children can be educated through such methods as briefings, checklists like those in the Appendix, and discussions that teach them about media bias. If our society is going to be warped enough to besiege its children with exploitive messages, the least we can do is arm them with healthy attitudes to help them withstand the assault.

To exert pressure for better health education, write to your state department of education and your local school district. Get the support of the PTA if possible. Try to work out programs where people with various beliefs may choose options for their children, perhaps through "levels" of sex education. This plan could begin with an already established and successful program, "Postponing Sexual Involvement."[105] Emphasize the concern we all have in common: the sexual safety and responsibility of our young people.

BE OF GOOD COURAGE

Don't expect immediate change in everything you attempt. Feel good right now that you're taking a stand. Be proud of yourself for that. It may take time for various inroads to be made, but they are beginning already.

IF YOU ADD YOUR VOICE

When you assert yourself or disagree in person with other people's opinions, you may feel embarrassed at first because of the people who are present. But you should feel proud. Remember the survivors and potential victims who are *not* there. For just as a friend thanks you for defending her in her absence, if you could hear the voices of millions of survivors, you would hear them say, *Thank you.* Thank you for speaking up so that what I have suffered may be even partially vindicated. Thank you for ensuring that all of us have less chance of being hurt in the future. *Thank you.*

Although I am a college professor and have tried to present objective data here, this book is not an academic treatise: *it is a formula for action.* I could not have written these words with such conviction had I not been fueled with the determination of a woman, a mother, a friend and loved one of survivors, and an American who cares that my society should endure and prosper.

It is not a favor to society when we speak up. It is our obligation. Those who will inherit our earth and our society deserve to be protected. I share the belief of Native Americans that the earth is a sacred trust, and we must leave it as safe as we found it. A healthy society is also a sacred trust—we should not allow it to be damaged. We owe to future generations a safe place in which to grow.

In the words of the Talmud,

I did not find this world desolate when I entered it.
My ancestors planted for me before I was born.
So do I plant for those who come after me.

APPENDIX:
WHERE TO GET AND GIVE HELP

Remember that you should apply basic good judgment in choosing an organization, agency, or therapist, or in deciding on actions to ensure your safety. You will need to take responsibility for checking out any sources listed here.

You may be able to call one of these sources to get information about others not listed. If you live in a small town and cannot find local resources, try the largest nearby city. It will help to have your list of questions by the phone when you call to ask about services, confidentiality, fees, etc.

Phone numbers of privately supported agencies can change frequently. In other cases phone lines jam quickly when complaints come in. Where these problems are likely to occur I have provided only the address of the agency.

PREVENTING SEXUAL AGGRESSION IN THE MEDIA

Organizations to Join

Here are two well-known groups working hard against exploitation. Neither group advocates censorship:

National Coalition on Television Violence
P.O. Box 2157
Champaign, IL 61824
Phone: 1-217-384-1920

Women Against Pornography
321 W. 47th St.
New York, NY 10036
Phone: 1-212-307-5055

There are also several other organizations that act as watchdog groups to urge changes in the media; most are religiously affiliated. To find one, ask your librarian.

Where to Send Protest Letters, Suggestions, or Complaints

> Complaints and Investigation Bureau,
> TV, Radio, and Cable Complaints
> Federal Communications Commission
> 2025 M Street NW, Room 8202
> Washington, D.C. 20554
> Phone: 1-202-632-7048

> Fox TV Center
> 5746 W. Sunset Blvd.
> Los Angeles, CA 90028

> NBC
> 30 Rockefeller Plaza
> New York, NY 10112

> CBS
> 51 W. 52nd St.
> New York, NY 10019

> ABC
> 47 W. 66th St.
> New York, NY 10023

Sample Protest Letter to Channel, Station, or Sponsor

A letter should be brief and might go something like this:

> Dear (sponsor, network, or local station),
>
> Yesterday I watched a program (or saw a commercial or an advertisement) (on your station, on your network, or sponsored by your company) that I found very offensive. It occurred on (date, time, station, channel) and it depicted (mention any kind of aggression to which you object).

Research shows that portraying _____ can be harmful, even to adults. In light of our serious national problems with these kinds of aggression and violence, I plan to boycott your (products, network, business) until such time as you cease to sponsor sexually exploitive or violent material.

Or: This is not the kind of programming that I want (my family) to watch. I hope that you upgrade your programming so that viewers can see exciting content that is not violent.

DISEASE PREVENTION AND BIRTH CONTROL

Sources of Information and/or Testing

These services should always be confidential, but you may want to double-check to feel reassured. There are some state laws requiring the reporting of certain STDs to keep track for health purposes.

Planned Parenthood has centers in most major cities in the United States and offers contraception and other services, depending on the center. Check your phone book for the number.

County health departments usually provide sites for testing and treatment for STDs. Look in your phone book or ask the operator. You may want to inquire about the people to whom the testing site reports results, and the confidentiality of those results, especially in testing for the HIV (AIDS) virus. There are some slight differences in the way this is handled, and HIV-positive individuals are rightly concerned about confidentiality.

AIDS prevention and AIDS support groups have sprung up in various locations and can refer you to testing sources. Check your phone book for AIDS agencies to get a referral.

HOTLINES

National STD Hotline: 1-800-227-8922

National AIDS Hotline: 1-800-342-AIDS
    For Hispanics: 1-800-344-SIDA

National Herpes Hotline: 1-919-361-2120

For a unique pamphlet about hygiene practices that can decrease the risk of STD, send one dollar to:

American Foundation for the
Prevention of Venereal Disease, Inc.
799 Broadway, Suite 638
New York, NY 10003

For information on how to use a condom correctly, or to learn about high- and low-risk behaviors for any STD:

Call government-sponsored testing sites listed under your county's health department, or Planned Parenthood.

Or: Call the STD or the AIDS hotline (above), or call your college health service.

In case of sexual harassment, the two major agencies are:

Equal Employment Opportunity Commission
(Check the government section of your phone book.)

Human Rights Commission
(Check your state capitol for the number.)

LEGAL ASSISTANCE FOR SEXUAL HARASSMENT AND SEXUAL ASSAULT

NAME	DESCRIPTION	HOW TO LOCATE
Title VII— Civil Rights Act	Federal legislation prohibiting sex discrimination in employment	EEOC: Equal Employment Opportunity Commission
State Civil Rights Laws	Similar to Title VII, but vary from state to state	Your state's human rights commission
Title IX— Education Amendments	Prohibits sex discrimination in education	OCR: Office of Civil Rights, Dept. of Education (regional offices)
Criminal Rape Statutes	Vary among states; some laws include degrees of sexual assault other than forcible rape. Apply *only* when actual assault occurs	Police or prosecuting attorney
Other Criminal Charges	Assault, battery, or intentional infliction of emotional harm	Police or prosecuting attorney
Civil Lawsuit	Private money damages, but very difficult to get unless actual physical assault	Private attorney
Workers Compensation	Some states beginning to recognize claims for emotional distress arising from sexual harassment by employer	Private attorney

HELP FOR CHILDREN

To report child abuse: Most states have a Child Abuse Hotline. To find yours, call information or the operator.

Or: Call the National Child Abuse Hotline, 1-800-422-4453

Runaways are often running from sexual abuse at home.

The National Runaway Switchboard: 1-800-621-4000
The National Runaway Hotline: 1-800-231-6946

HELP FOR VIOLENCE AT HOME

Domestic Violence Hotline: 1-800-333-SAFE (7233)
Hearing impaired call: 1-800-873-6363

HELP FOR ALCOHOL
AND DRUG ABUSE

For the alcoholic/addict, check in your phone book or in the next largest town for:

National Council on Alcohol and Drug Abuse
Alcoholics Anonymous
Narcotics Anonymous

For family or a friend of someone affected by alcohol and/or drug abuse, call:

Al-Anon
Alateen

If you do not find the number in the phone book, call your local Alcoholics Anonymous chapter.

Drug hotlines

Al-Anon Family Group Headquarters: 1-800-356-9996
There is also a Cocaine Hotline which answers questions and provides treatment referrals: 1-800-COCAINE.
The National Institute on Drug Abuse has a Drug Abuse Information and Referral Line: 1-800-662-4357

HELP FOR SURVIVORS OF SEXUAL EXPLOITATION

In big cities you should look in the phone book for the people who could most logically refer you for help: the rape crisis hotline, or any kind of women's center (which is often on a college or university campus). They may know where to refer male survivors as well. If you're in a small town, call long distance; many women's centers will let you reverse the charges.

Incest

Two organizations that help provide support groups nationwide for incest survivors:

> Survivors of Incest Anonymous
> P.O. Box 21817
> Baltimore, MD 21222-6817
> Phone: 1-301-282-3400

> Incest Survivors Anonymous
> P.O. Box 5613
> Long Beach, CA 90805-0613
> Phone: 1-213-428-5599

Several books are available for survivors. Ask one of the above groups for suggestions.

Preventing and Treating Rape

Rape crisis hotlines exist in all major cities. They are sometimes listed as a "crisis hotline." Ask the operator for the number, or call a county- or state-run counseling department. If you are in a small town, get the information operator in a large city and call a crisis hotline long distance; they may let you call collect.

Your Personal Safety Checklist to Prevent Stranger Rape:

Check those things you do routinely:

At Home

___ I refuse to admit anyone to my home or apartment whom I do not know or was not expecting.

___ I always ask to see proper identification through a closed door or peephole.

___ I leave the door open if a properly identified repairman enters, and plan where I will go if the situation becomes threatening.

___ I list my name by initials only on my mailbox and in the phone book.

___ I always keep my doors and windows locked.

___ I use timers to turn on lights and radio if I expect to be out all day.

___ I have the key ready before I approach my car or my home.

___ I have adequate lighting at all doors.

___ I have a phone by my bed.

___ I vary my routine a little each day if I have to be in a risky area.

___ I do not allow strangers to use my phone.

In the Car

___ I keep my car, tires, etc., in good condition to prevent breakdown.

___ I keep my car doors and windows locked at all times.

___ I travel on well-lighted streets where people are always around.

___ I have plans to stay in my car if it breaks down.

___ I carry a SEND HELP sign.

___ I have a quarter taped to a card with a tow truck number so I can pass it through a slightly opened window.

__ I keep the car in gear while waiting at a stop sign.

__ I check the rearview mirror occasionally and know where to find police, fire station, or other safe place if I am followed.

__ I remember to sound the horn if I need to get attention.

__ I try to park my car where it is well lighted at night.

__ I lock my car at all times and look inside before unlocking it.

__ Whenever possible, at night I walk out of shopping centers, work, or other places along with other people.

In Public Places

__ I use drugs little if at all; my drug use allows me to remain in control.

__ I drive my own car or arrange a ride so I needn't depend on someone I do not know well.

__ If I am harassed by a person in a public place such as a bar, I report him to the owner, bouncer, or bartender.

__ I walk near the street and avoid places such as alleys, doorways, or shrubbery where someone could hide.

__ If a driver pulls over to ask directions, I call them out briefly from a safe distance away.

__ I do not hitchhike under any circumstances.

__ I do not walk alone at night.

__ I wear shoes that allow me to run if necessary.

__ I am prepared to approach a house for help.

__ I carry a loud siren, a whistle, or a buzzer for attracting attention in an emergency.

__ I am prepared, if a car approaches me and the driver threatens me, to scream and run in the *opposite* direction from the car.

__ I walk with my head up and with confidence as if I know where I am going.

__ If I find myself on an elevator with someone who seems risky, I get off at the next floor; if such a person enters an elevator I am planning to enter, I wait until the empty elevator returns.

__ I always stand near the control panel on an elevator so I can reach the alarm if necessary.

Immediately After a Rape:

1. Don't change anything about your body—don't wash or even comb your hair. Leave your clothes as they are. You could destroy evidence.

2. Strongly consider reporting the incident to police. You may prevent another woman from being assaulted, and you will be taking charge, starting on the path from victim to survivor.

3. Ask a relative or friend to take you to a hospital; if you can't, get an ambulance or a police car. If you call the hospital, tell them why you're requesting an ambulance in case they might send someone trained in rape crisis.

4. Seeking help is an assertive way to show you're worth it. Seek medical help. Injuries of which you are unaware may be detected. Insist that a written or photographic record be made documenting your condition. You may decide that you're going to prosecute, and you'll need evidence.

5. You have medical rights. Ask questions. Ask what's available to you, ask for what you need to make you comfortable. You are calling the shots now. Ask for confidentiality if that's what you want. Refuse what you don't want.

A Book for Rape Survivors:

If You Are Raped by Kathryn M. Johnson (Holmes Beach, Florida: Learning Publications, 1985). There are other books available. Ask your local library or bookstore.

SOURCES OF HELP FOR SEX OFFENDERS

Society is only now beginning to confront the need for treatment of sex offenders. There are a number of treatment concepts, ranging from the view that the individual needs psychotherapy from a professional, to the view that the person suffers from a sexual addiction and needs a Twelve Step program similar to that of AA. Those wanting to begin with individual or group psychotherapy may want to consult a therapist who is certified by the American Association of Sex Educators, Counselors, and Therapists. Those desiring a Twelve Step program and group support, or lacking the funds for professional treatment, may write the following organizations or look for them in their local phone books:

Organizations:

Write the national offices for information about the closest group:

Sex Addicts Anonymous
P.O. Box 3038
Minneapolis, MN 55403

Sexaholics Anonymous (Sex Addiction)
P.O. Box 300
Simi Valley, CA 93062

Helpful Books:

Out of the Shadows: Understanding Sexual Addiction, by Patrick Carnes, Ph. D. (Minneapolis: CompCare, 1983).

Contrary to Love: Helping the Sexual Addict, by Patrick Carnes, Ph.D. (Minneapolis: CompCare, 1989).

IF YOU NEED PSYCHOTHERAPY

Good counseling or psychotherapy can improve your self-esteem, and help you recover from past traumatic experiences and reach your best potential. This effort may require a search on your part. If you've been victimized by a man, you may want to start with a woman therapist and vice versa. Try asking for a referral from one of the following:

- a crisis hotline
- a women's center on a college or university campus
- a local mental health association
- a counselor at your high school or college
- one of the other contacts listed in this Appendix

Don't continue with the first counselor you meet if you have major doubts about the person. The counselor should be supportive, yet try to help you to become self-sufficient so you can deal with your problems constructively. Look for a professional therapist with credentials at the master's degree level or beyond, and experience. An emotionally stable therapist welcomes questions about training or qualifications. She may be accredited by organizations where you could double-check credentials. The therapist should be objective—not a friend, not a lover. She should do more than just *listen*; she should help *you* to be the active problem-solver in your life. Don't be afraid to get a second opinion from another therapist if you are not sure you've chosen someone suitable for you. Some people work better with certain kinds of clients.

PLACES TO CALL FOR FURTHER REFERRALS

A number you can call for many kinds of referrals:

National Self-Help Clearinghouse: 1-212-642-2944

For example, if you want to find a national support group you could call NSHC.

United Way (or United Fund) in many major cities often has a referral number that connects people with sources of help for all kinds of problems. Look in your phone book.

MEDIA CHECKLISTS

To see how much sexual exploitation or other aggression is depicted in your favorite media, use the following checklists:

Sexual Messages in Media—Checklist

During a single program or film, or while looking at a magazine, check any of the following that occur:

__1. Characters show hostility by calling names or insulting the opposite sex.

__2. Characters manipulate and play games in love relationships; that is, they are deceptive:

    __they lie to their spouses about sex.

    __they lie to get sex from someone.

    __they otherwise deceive a sex partner.

__3. One gender dominates the other (use of power).

__4. Jokes or put-downs about commitment (such as jokes about how bad marriage is).

__5. Couple has intercourse without mention of birth control.

__6. Couple has intercourse occurring without mention of disease risk.

__7. Men or women make uninvited remarks about the secondary sex characteristics (breasts, etc.) of another person.

__8. Characters have titillating attitude about sex (making sexual implications out of events that are really not sexual) or they giggle about double meanings of words that could be interpreted as sexual.

__9. Men or women publicly put down the sexual abilities of another person.

__10. Character laughs at serious sexual problems (comedies that joke about unwed parenthood, deception, disease, prostitution, etc.).

__11. Women or men are consistently portrayed as stupid.

__12. An employer or fellow employee makes sexual remarks to another employee, or engages in more serious sexual harassment.

__13. Characters engage in sexual aggression or violence irrelevant to the plot (ranging from insults to rape).

__14. Males are portrayed as insensitive.

__15. Males are portrayed as more interested in sexual conquests than in the woman's feelings.

__16. Women are portrayed as weak or frightened.

__17. Women are portrayed as not really minding sexual force, or as liking it.

__18. Rape is attempted (regardless of whether victim began to like it).

__19. A completed rape was shown, whether graphically or not.

__20. Program or film implies rape myths:

   __women are always interested in sex.

   __men cannot help but be sex-driven.

   __other rape myths: _____.

__21. Other forms of sexual aggression or exploitation:

_____

_____

_____

_____

_____

_____

Aggression in Media—Checklist

During a single program or film, or while looking at a magazine, check any of the following that occur:

Verbal Aggression (people say things aimed at hurting someone):

__sarcasm (characters show anger through their tone of voice)

__threats (about psychological or physical harm that one character may carry out)

__screaming or yelling at another person, rather than talking to him respectfully

__making remarks that degrade or put down another person, or group

__telling untrue and destructive things behind a person's back

__frightening someone anonymously (such as over the telephone)

__other verbal aggression:_____

Nonverbal (Physical) Aggression

__smashing or destroying objects

__pushing or shoving

__shooting with a weapon

__poisoning

__stabbing

__war (justified, approved aggression). Describe how the people were hurt: _____

__using a car to hurt a person

__miscellaneous aggression: drowning, strangling, tripping, pushing off cliff, etc. Describe: _____

__other physical aggression: _____

Did the media present this violence realistically and sensitively, indicating that it harmed a human being? ____

OR:

Was it presented in a glorified way, irrelevant to the storyline, or less serious and tragic than it warranted? ____

Do you feel that you reacted the same way to the violence you saw as you would have seeing it on the screen for the first time? _____

After writing this checklist, did you become any more aware of anything about aggression and violence in the media? If so, what? _____

INDEX

END NOTES

1. "A Little Less Time For TV," *U.S. News and World Report,* 19 June 1989, 74.
2. "Tune In Tomorrow," *St. Louis Post-Dispatch,* 25 June, 2 July, 9 July, 16 July, 23 July 1989, sec. C.
3. Jackie Collins, *Rock Star* (New York: Simon and Schuster, 1988), 46.
4. Advertisement in *Vogue,* October 1988, p. 34. Ad reads: "Copyright by Revlon, Inc. Trouble is a trademark of Revlon, Inc."
5. United States Merit System Protection Board, *Sexual Harassment in the Federal Workplace: Is It A Problem?* (Washington, D.C.: Government Printing Office, 1981).
6. William H. Masters, Virginia E. Johnson, and Robert C. Kolodny, *Human Sexuality* (Boston: Scott, Foresman, and Co., 1988), 493.
7. Patricia Jakubowski and Arthur J. Lange, *The Assertive Option* (Champaign, Illinois: Research Press, 1978),161–64.
8. Frederick S. Perls, *Gestalt Therapy Verbatim* (Lafayette, California: The Real People Press, 1969), 1-4.
9. David Wheeler, "College Students Put Sex Partners at Risk of AIDS by Lying about Past Experiences," *Chronicle of Higher Education* (21 March 1990); Daniel Goleman, "The Lies Men Tell Put Women in Danger of AIDS," *New York Times,* 14 August 1988.
10. David Burns, *Feeling Good: the New Mood Therapy* (New York: New American Library, 1980), 234.
11. Thomas Harris, *I'm OK—You're OK* (New York: Harper and Row, 1967); Eric Berne, *Games People Play* (NewYork: Grove Press, 1964).
12. Albert Ellis and R.A. Harper, *A New Guide to Rational Living* (N. Hollywood, California: Wilshire Book Company, 1978).
13. Robert Allard, "Beliefs about AIDS as Determinants of Preventive Practices and of Support for Coercive Measures," *American Journal of Public Health* 79, no. 4 (April 1989): 448.
14. Sol Gordon and Judith Gordon, *Raising a Child Conservatively in a Sexually Permissive World* (New York: Simon and Schuster, 1983), 23.
15. Jeffrey A. Kelly and Janet S. St. Lawrence, *Behavioral Group Intervention to Teach AIDS Risk Reduction Skills* (Jackson, Mississippi: University of Mississippi Medical School, 1990), 43.
16. David Spiegel and Herbert Spiegel, *Trance and Treatment: Clinical Uses of Hypnosis* (New York: Basic Books, 1978), 215.
17. Thomas E. Radecki, ed., *NCTV News* 11, nos. 3–5 (April–June, 1990):3.
18. Danielle Steele, *Going Home* (New York: Pocket Books, 1973), 19–20.
19. Sol Gordon, *Seduction Lines Heard 'Round the World and Answers You Can Give* (Buffalo, New York: Prometheus Books, 1987).
20. Kelly and St. Lawrence, *Behavioral Group Intervention,* 43.

21. Gayle M. Stringer and Deanna Rants-Rodriguez, *So What's It To Me? Sexual Assault Information for Guys* (Renton, Washington: King County Rape Relief, 1987), 10.

22. Don Jackson and J. H. Weakland, "Conjoint Family Therapy: Some Considerations on Theory, Technique, and Results," in *Changing Families*, ed. Jay Haley (New York: Grune & Stratton, 1971), 16.

23. By permission in a letter from Nicole Hollander, 7-25-90.

24. Kelly and St. Lawrence, *Behavioral Group Intervention*.

25. Margaret Davis, *Lovers, Doctors, and the Law* (New York: Harper and Row, 1988), 22–23.

26. Barbara A. Gutek, *Sex and the Workplace* (San Francisco: Jossey-Bass Publishers, 1985), 58.

27. United States Merit Systems Protection Board, *Sexual Harassment in the Federal Workplace: Is It A Problem?* (Washington, D.C.: Government Printing Office, 1981).

28. Ronni Sandross, "Sexual Harassment in the Fortune 500," *Working Woman* 13 (December 1988): 69.

29. Gutek, *Sex and the Workplace*, 56–57.

30. Billie W. Dziech and Linda Weiner, *The Lecherous Professor: Sexual Harassment on Campus* (Boston: Beacon Press, 1984); Gutek, *Sex in the Workplace*.

31. Dziech and Weiner, *Lecherous Professor*, 13–14.

32. Antonia Abbey, "Sex Differences in Attributions for Friendly Behavior: Do Males Misperceive Females' Friendliness?" *Journal of Personality and Social Psychology* 42, no. 5 (May 1982): 830.

33. Elissa Clarke, *Stopping Sexual Harassment: A Handbook* (Detroit: Labor and Education Research Project, 1981), 12.

34. Interview with Lois Vander Waerdt, President, the Employment Partnership, September 26, 1990.

35. Mary Rowe, "Dealing With Sexual Harassment," *Harvard Business Review* 59, no. 3 (May–June 1981): 42.

36. Interview with Lois Vander Waerdt.

37. Peter Rutter, *Sex in the Forbidden Zone* (Los Angeles: Jeremy P. Tarcher, 1989), 22–23.

38. dell fitzgerald-richards, *the rape journal* (Oakland, Calif.: Women's Press Collective, 1974).

39. "Women under Assault," *Newsweek*, 16 July 1990, 23.

40. Peggy R. Sanday, "The Socio-cultural Context of a Rape: A Cross-cultural Study," *The Journal of Social Issues* 37 (1981): 5.

41. Robin Warshaw, *I Never Called It Rape* (New York: Harper and Row, 1988), 33.

42. D. D. Smith, "The Social Content of Pornography," *Journal of Communication* 26 (1976): 16.

43. P. E. Dietz and B. Evans, "Pornographic Imagery and Prevalence of Paraphilia," *American Journal of Psychiatry* 139 (1982): 1493.

44. Fred M. Stewart, *Century* (New York: New American Library, 1981), 245.

45. N. M. Malamuth and Edward Donnerstein, eds., *Pornography and Sexual Aggression* (New York: Academic Press, 1984).

46. Mary P. Koss, Christine A. Gidycz, and Nadine Wisniewski, "The Scope of Rape: Incidence and Prevalence of Sexual Aggression and Victimization in a National Sample of Higher Education Students," *Journal of Consulting and Clinical Psychology* 55, no. 2 (1987): 162.

47. "'Date Rape' Stirring Debate at Mizzou," *St. Louis Post-Dispatch*, 23 April 1989.

48. "Campus Debates Rape Survey Conclusions," *St. Louis Post-Dispatch*, 12 February 1990.

49. Malamuth and Donnerstein, *Pornography and Sexual Aggression*.

50. Antonia Abbey, "Sex Differences in Attributions for Friendly Behavior: Do Males Misperceive Females' Friendliness?" *Journal of Personality and Social Psychology* 42, no. 5 (1982): 830; D. N. Lipton, E. C. McDonnel, and R. M. McFall, "Heterosexual Perception in Rapists," *Journal of Consulting and Clinical Psychology* 55, no. 1 (1987): 17.

51. N. M. Malamuth, "Rape Proclivity among Males," *Journal of Social Issues* 37 (1981): 138.

52. Virginia Greendlinger and Donn Byrne, "Coercive Sexual Fantasies of College Men and Predictors of Self-reported Likelihood to Rape and Overt Sexual Aggression," *Journal of Sex Research* 23 (1987): 1.

53. Warshaw, *I Never Called It Rape*.

54. Susan Forward and Joan Torres, *Men Who Hate Women and the Women Who Love Them* (New York: Bantam Books, 1986).

55. E. Sandra Byers, Barbara L. Giles, and Dorothy L. Price, "Definiteness and Effectiveness of Women's Responses to Unwanted Sexual Advances," *Basic and Applied Social Psychology* 8, no. 4 (1987): 321.

56. "Rape: The Macho View," quoting the research of D. L. Mosher and R. D. Anderson, *Psychology Today* 21 (April 1987): 12.

57. Judith M. Siegel, Susan B. Sorenson, Jacqueline M. Golding, M. Audrey Burnam, and Judith A. Stein, "Resistance to Sexual Assault: Who Resists and What Happens? *American Journal of Public Health* 79, no. 1 (January 1989): 27.

58. Joyce Levine-McCombie and Mary P. Koss, "Acquaintance Rape: Effective Avoidance Strategies," *Psychology of Women Quarterly* 10 (1986): 311.

59. Siegel et al. "Resistance to Sexual Assault."

60. Pauline B. Bart and Patricia H. O'Brien, *Stopping Rape* (New York: Pergamon Press, 1985).

61. Charlene L. Muehlenard, Debra E. Friedman, and Celeste M. Thomas, "Is Date Rape Justifiable?" *Psychology of Women Quarterly* 9, no. 3 (1985): 297.

62. Siegel et al. "Resistance to Sexual Assault."

63. Doris Lessing, *The Memoirs of a Survivor* (New York: Bantam Books, 1976), 14.

64. David Finkelhor, *Sexually Victimized Children* (New York: The Free Press, 1979), 53.

65. Carol Cassell and Pamela Wilson, *Sexuality Education: A Resource Book* (New York: Garland, 1989), 7.

66. Masters, Johnson, and Kolodny, *Human Sexuality*, 450.

67. Margaret Mead, "A Proposal: We Need Taboos on Sex at Work," *Redbook* no. 6 (April 1978): 31, 33, 38.

68. Susan Gubar and Joan Hoff, *For Adult Users Only* (Bloomington, Indiana: Indiana University Press, 1989), 90.

69. *Attorney General's Commission on Pornography, Final Report* (Washington, D.C.: U.S. Department of Justice, July 1986), 324–26.

70. As discussed in Edward Donnerstein, Daniel Linz, and Steven Penrod, *The Question of Pornography* (New York: The Free Press, 1987): 118.

71. Daniel Linz, "Sexual Violence in the Media: Effects on Male Viewers and Implications for Society" (unpublished doctoral dissertation, University of Wisconsin, 1985); Daniel Linz, Edward Donnerstein, and Steven Penrod, "The Effects of Multiple Exposures of Filmed Violence against Women," *Journal of Communication* 34 (1984): 130.

72. Dolf Zillmann, "Effects of Prolonged Consumption of Pornography," in *Pornography: Research Advances and Policy Considerations*, ed. Dolf Zillmann and Jennings Bryant (Hillsdale, N.J.: Lawrence Erlbaum Associates, 1989), 127–57.

73. Sanday, "Socio-cultural Context of Rape."

74. "Women Lament Loss of Roles," *St. Louis Post-Dispatch*, 10 August, 1990.

75. Ni Yang and Daniel Linz, "Movie Ratings and the Content of Adult Videos: The Sex-Violence Ratio," *Journal of Communication* 40, no. 2 (Spring 1990): 28.

76. "Married With Children" episode shown at 8 P.M. Sunday, July 22, 1990. Channel 30, St. Louis, Missouri.

77. L. Sabin, "Why I Threw Out My TV Set," *Today's Health* (February 1972): 70-71; F. J. Prial, "Cable TV Is Said to Top Networks in Movie Violence," *New York Times*, 22 January 1983.

78. Radecki, *NCTV News*, 8.

79. As reported in "Women under Assault," *Newsweek*, 16 July 1990, 24.

80. Diana E. H. Russell, *Sexual Exploitation* (Newbury Park, California: Sage Library of Social Research, 1984), 124.

81. W. L. Marshall, "Pornography and Sex Offenders," in *Pornography: Research Advances and Policy Considerations*, ed. Dolf Zillmann and Jennings Bryant (Hillsdale, N.J.: Lawrence Erlbaum Associates, 1989), 185–214.

82. *Forbes* 146, no. 3, 6 August 1990.

83. N. M. Malamuth and Edward Donnerstein, eds., *Pornography and Sexual Aggression* (New York: Academic Press, 1984); Donnerstein, Linz, and Penrod, *The Question of Pornography*; Zillmann and Bryant, eds., *Pornography: Research Advances.*

84. Dolf Zillmann and Jennings Bryant, eds., "Effects of Massive Exposure to Pornography," in Donnerstein, Linz, and Penrod, *The Question of Pornography*, 75–76.

85. Dolf Zillmann and James B. Weaver, "Pornography and Men's Sexual Callousness toward Women," in Zillman and Bryant, eds., *Pornography: Research Advances*, 95–125.

86. Dolf Zillmann, "Effects of Prolonged Consumption of Pornography," in Zillman and Bryant, eds., *Pornography: Research Advances*, 153–55. This paper is an updated version of a paper commissioned by the Surgeon General for the Surgeon General's Workshop on Pornography and Public Health, 1986.

87. Donnerstein, Linz, and Penrod, *The Question of Pornography*, 158.

88. Warshaw, *I Never Called It Rape*.

89. D. L. Mosher and M. Sirkin, "Measuring a Macho Personality Constellation," *Journal of Research in Personality* 18 (1984): 150.

90. As reported in Zillmann and Weaver, "Pornography and Men's Sexual Callousness toward Women," Zillmann and Bryant, eds., *Pornography: Research Advances*, 102.

91. Ibid., 104.

92. Dolf Zillmann, J. B. Weaver, N. Mundorf, and C. F. Aust, "Effects of the Opposite-gender Companion's Affect to Horror or Distress, Delight and Attraction," *Journal of Personality and Social Psychology* 51 (1986): 586.

93. From a union protest song of the same title. Copyright 1947, People's Songs, Inc., in *Songs of Work and Freedom* (Garden City, New York: Doubleday and Company, 1960), 54.

94. Edward Donnerstein and Daniel Linz, University of California at Santa Barbara, personal communication with Donnerstein, January 9, 1991.

95. Radecki, *NCTV News*.

96. John N. Baker, "Publisher Responsibility and Bret Easton Ellis," *Publishers Weekly*, 30 November 1990, 7.

97. "As Nasty as They Wanna Be," Luke Records, PAC JAM Publishing (BMI), Liberty City, Florida.

98. Radecki, *NCTV News*, 2.

99. Ibid., 14.

100. Ibid., 6.

101. Daniel Linz, C. W. Turner, B. W. Hesse, and S. D. Penrod, "Bases of Liability for Injuries Produced by Media Portrayals of Violent Pornography," in *Pornography and Sexual Aggression*, Malamuth and Donnerstein, eds., 277–304.

102. J. V. P. Check and N. M. Malamuth, "Can Exposure to Pornography Have Positive Effects?" Paper presented at the annual meeting of the American Psychological Association, Los Angeles, August 1981.

103. Donnerstein, Linz, and Malamuth, *The Question of Pornography*, 195–96.

104. Telephone interview, July 19, 1990.

105. Information on this program can be obtained from Grady Memorial Hospital, Emory/Grady Teen Services Program, Hospital Box 26158, 80 Butler Street S.E., Atlanta, Georgia, 30335.

ABOUT THE AUTHOR

Elizabeth Powell, a psychologist with an M.S. degree in Clinical Psychology and an M.A. degree in Family Counseling, teaches at a large urban community college. She assumes that anyone who grows up in American society learns unhealthy attitudes about sex, and that consequently sexual assertiveness must be taught. Her students therefore analyze violent and exploitive messages on television. Using role-plays and video tapes, they learn behavioral skills that help prevent problems involving pressure and coercion.

Powell has been honored several times as a Master Teacher. A member of the National Education Association and the American Association of Sex Educators, Counselors, and Therapists, she often speaks at professional meetings about the teaching techniques she has developed in her classroom.

Elizabeth Powell now heads the AIDS task force at her college and appears frequently on radio and television to speak about sexuality and AIDS.